Dodging the Bullets

Dodging the Bullets

A Disaster Preparation Guide
for
Joomla!™ Web Sites

Tom Canavan

iUniverse, Inc.
New York Lincoln Shanghai

Dodging the Bullets
A Disaster Preparation Guide for Joomla!™ Web Sites

iUniverse, Inc.

iUniverse books may be ordered through booksellers or by contacting:

iUniverse
2021 Pine Lake Road, Suite 100
Lincoln, NE 68512
www.iuniverse.com
1-800-Authors (1-800-288-4677)

ISBN: 978-0-595-43956-0 (pbk)
ISBN: 978-0-595-88276-2 (ebk)

Printed in the United States of America

To my Wife Carol Ann

I could not have done this without you

I love you

Table of Contents

Foreword

For me, it was a winter of discontent. As the mercury dropped and the weather cooled, so too did hundreds of Joomla!™-based sites drop off the Internet landscape, victims of techno-terrorism. This was a community in crisis, and as with any crisis, human nature has a need to make sense of what has happened, why it has happened and who is to blame.

Site defacements and remote attacks could be considered faceless crimes perpetrated by unknown assailants, as it's often very difficult to trace the true origins of the attack. In this climate, it's often easier to focus one's attention on the software flaw that allowed the attack to occur, and hence the developers.

But there will always be crises from which we must recover, and dwelling on negatives like blame robs us of growing from the experience. In my own lifetime, I've lived through the Brisbane (Australia) floods, and have seen Darwin virtually wiped off the map after cyclone Tracy. These were seminal moments that gave me an appreciation of disaster management in times of crisis. Later in my professional career I was involved in the development of community disaster management plans, which gave me an insight into the multi-faceted nature of crises.

The Chinese represent the word "crisis" by joining two ideograms together, which individually represent the concepts of "danger" and "opportunity". Crises in whatever form are turning points in our lives. There is the danger of death and there is the opportunity for growth.

Death doesn't necessarily mean in the physical sense though. When we're talking about Joomla!™-based sites, it could be the death of your site's search engine popularity, or it could be the death of your business. The opportunity presented by a crisis is to grow from one's experience, so that you're able to avoid future crises, or in the event that you can't avoid them, you have the knowledge, skills, and mechanisms in place to minimize their impact.

Being one of the many who had their web sites defaced, I was fortunate to know Tom, who had been monitoring the crisis as it unfolded. Tom saw the average Joomla!™ site administrator had a desperate need for information on how to prevent, and respond to a site crisis, and put fingers to keyboard in order to share his wealth of knowledge. My good fortune was that I had the privilege of reading through Tom's early manuscripts at a time when my own sites were under attack. The insights I gained into server management have helped to keep my sites up and running, in spite of being hit hundreds of times daily by remote attacks. I'm sure you'll also find Tom's book is a valuable resource that will improve your site management practices, and always be close at hand as you go about your daily Internet activities.

Kathy Strickland (AKA PixelBunyiP)—www.raptorservices.com.au/

Preface

Disaster preparedness is a topic that should be foremost in the mind of any Joomla!™ site administrator. The terrain of major corporations for disaster recovery, and business continuance, has been shoved into the minds of every American and, for that matter, the world. The events of the 9–11 terrorist attacks in the United States, the devastation of Hurricane Katrina, and the horrific events of the Tsunamis that the Asia Pacific region suffered under have galvanized our thinking towards true disaster preparedness.

These three events alone should give pause for thought, and cause you to ask, "what if?" What if my e-commerce site went down? In the grand scheme of world events, this may seem unimportant. To you it could mean not staying in business.

The purpose of this book

This book is written specifically for site administrators of Joomla!™-based websites as a guide to prepare for disaster. The disaster may come in the form of a hurricane or from a cracker exploit. Additionally hardware and operating systems failures account for a majority of issues reported in technical infrastructures. This book is intended to help you prepare and respond in a timely fashion. In a nutshell, this book will help you establish good maintenance practices, backup/restoration procedures, and will help you to gather the critical information needed to prepare a response.

It will provide you with a proper and concise method to report incidents to the Joomla!™ community, the wider Internet community, ISP's, and your web hosting provider.

Many good books have been written that take the subject of disaster preparation and recovery in greater scope than this book. However I did not write this as a comprehensive guide to full disaster recovery planning, but a focused view on preparing your Joomla!™ sites for disaster.

Terminology and style of this book

This guide requires only basic administration skills to implement and execute a plan of action. The style of writing is free from most "buzz-word" type terms, or the ever-deadly three letter acronym (TLA) wherever possible.

My background includes over twenty years with computer vendors such as Dell, AST Research and Texas Instruments, working with CIO's, CTO's and the technical staffs of the Fortune 100 companies. This position gave me access to many different customers, scenarios, knowledge, experience as well as unique, in-depth training and hands on experience in order to bring you this book.

I wrote this to be a working book, one that can be written in, marked up and kept for reference. It has been printed in paperback for that reason. When you arrive at a form in the book, fill it out as this is the intended use.

Your plan is not something eight inches thick to reside on a shelf somewhere to gather dust. No, your plan is a living, breathing document; one that will require some regular attention.

Like anything that receives regular positive attention, it will be ready for use when the dark cloud of a disastrous event occurs.

"Event"

When you see the word "event" in the text this means any event that has caused disruption to your site and needs to be addressed. This can include virus, cracker, weather, power, hardware failure, and more. I do not presume, except where appropriate a specific event.

Some things not covered in this book.

This book is not a complete guide to facility, work space, people evacuation, network, voice, fire suppression, flooding, or data line restoration. Those are beyond the scope of this book.

I wish you Godspeed in life and a site with five nines of uptime and availability.

Acknowledgements

There are many people who helped me along the way in the conception, design and ultimately the development of this book. I want to take a moment to recognize their efforts and dedication to this project.

First, a giant thanks to my wife Carol who supported me 'above and beyond the call of duty' during this book effort. Mr. Michael Gray for helping me think through the 'non-Joomla!™' portions. Mr. Jeff Mullaney, a good friend from "two-lives" in the computer industry, for his detailed review of my grammar, thoughts and ideas. Mr. Chuck Gilbert for listening to me and helping me hash out the backup and recovery portions of the book. Mrs. Kathy Strickland, my co-host on www.joomlajabber.com for the countless hours reviewing the early manuscripts and for convincing me to write this. Mr. Pascal Nemmar for providing the insight of physical 'security' issues. Mr. John Rittinghouse for all his years of friendship and guidance in security matters. Mr. Rick Kaczmarek, for being Mr. RED PEN over the years helping me hone my writing skills. Mr. Rob Hamilton for spending time reviewing and discussing the book. Mr. Tony Moon for introducing me to Joomla!™ and providing the outline on describing permissions. Mr. Mark Turner, CIO of ABC Radio, Inc, for reviewing the book for usefulness and clarity of purpose. Mr. Simon Tatham for his permission to include "How to report bugs effectively." Supporting cast members to this effort such as www.bigstockphoto.com for having wonderful illustrations and photos and for permission to include them in this book. The Joomla!™ Core team for delivering the product and the community for their collective wisdom. And as odd as it may sound, the 'crackers', malcontents and evil doers on the Internet who started attacking Joomla!™ sites all over the world. Without your negative activity and force, I would not have thought to write this book. Thanks to www.iuniverse.com for having the incredible technology from which to publish this book.

Introduction

What is valued in war is victory
What is not is prolonged operations
And the general who understands
How to employ troops is the
Minister of the people's fate
And the arbiter of the nations destiny

Sun Tzu—The Art of War

W hy should you read this book? Is it worth your time? Will you gain valuable knowledge? What benefits will your site, or your customers expect? It can be answered like this: *If you do not have a disaster preparation plan, then you need one.* Plain and simple your Joomla!™-based website is worth it and so are you.

Using this book will help you craft an emergency response plan to disasters. Think about it, if you are a small business you should be online with a web presence. And therefore you should have a plan to protect that website from the unseen future.

If you run a traditional brick and mortar store front you probably have an alarm, maybe a fire suppression system, or fire extinguisher, you lock the doors, and you might even have security cameras. *Why is your website immune from having similar safeguards?*

In this book you will learn how to establish a *baseline* for your site, enabling you to quickly recover from an attack or incident. We delve deeply into the ideas and methods of fortifying your site against common threats. In fact as this introduction was being written a new round of attacks has starting occurring on Joomla!™-based sites. It is too early to determine the true nature of the threat, however it is never too early to prepare.

Should you need to report an incident, a bug, or ask for help, included is a detailed chapter on incident reporting. By reporting problems in this fashion you will have the dual benefit of getting your problem resolved while adding strength through knowledge to the community.

Anytime someone is asked to document something in writing, it will be written in a style that fits their mindset, but may not make sense to anyone else. In your disaster preparedness plan, you must have your documentation standardized to allow anyone to pick it up, and do a restore or backup. Provided with this book is numerous forms designed for every activity around backup, recovery, testing, deployment, and who is allowed to do what.

Do you remember going through fire-safety drills at school? Why this was done is obvious, it was to prepare you to act as calmly as possible under stress of a real fire. This book will guide you through the steps to conduct, document, and improve your plan through disaster preparation drills. By working through this plan you and your team will know their roles, will understand what to do, and will be able to respond when there is real pressure.

Finally, if you want your fifteen minutes of fame, you may just get it; but be prepared. Most of us have not dealt with the media, only we sit by, and absorb their output. Should you ever be faced with a reporter wanting to talk about your outage, you can be prepared and ready by having your own media communication plan. The book closes with a full chapter on designing your communications plan to have as part of your disaster preparation.

I asked at the start of this section *why read this book*? Is it worth the time required? I believe it to be and I believe once you take the journey through, you will agree.

I want to thank you for purchasing this book that is designed to help you to craft your site disaster preparation plan. The principles laid out in this book are time-tested and should serve you well. Keep in mind that as you finish this book, simply placing the binder on the shelf won't help; using the book will help keep your site up and running.

When you conduct your first drill, your plan, may very likely fail. This is not a factor of a poor plan, but rather the symptom of a 'first-time' plan effect. Without a doubt, no matter how carefully, and correctly you plan, on your first drill you will find holes.

Do not despair, simply go back through the plan, check your notes, fix the holes and then get back at it.

Keep in mind that these forms are subject to change with your input. Please drop a note by visiting www.joomspyder.com. Any and all suggestions are welcome and if we implement your suggestions we will add them to the forms for download. If you have a success please let us hear from you as well.

Tom Canavan

book@joomspyder.com

January 2007

Chapter 1

Waiting for Mr. Murphy

'if it can go wrong, it will'

Why read this chapter?

The concept of disaster preparedness and business continuance planning is rarely part of any small business and yet it should be.

This chapter introduces you to some foundational principles of disaster preparedness.

Learning goals in this chapter

- Define risk tolerance for your site
- Assessing risk in your site
- Determining the affordability of your plan
- Gain a working understanding of failure response

Waiting for Mr. Murphy

There are six types of ill-fated armies:
Running off, Lax,
Sinking, Crumbling
Chaotic and routed.
These disasters are not brought by
Heaven and Earth but
By the Generals errors.

Sun Tzu—The Art of War

Often when calamity such as an attack on your site or a failure of the hardware on a server there are two reactions on the part of those in charge. One is the response of the experienced administrator who remains calm, collected, and addresses the problems. The other is the bad administrators—those who are too lazy or scattered. Those who bury their heads in the sand and ignore their sites until it is too late. They are simply sinking, blaming everything and everyone else for their failures. This chapter introduces you to the concept of risk tolerance. Risk tolerance is an assessment of how much down time you can tolerate without crossing the point of no return and destroying your business. Learning how to assess your risk is as important as planning for it. With any plan and especially a disaster preparedness' plan there is a financial component that is needed to prepare for disaster. This may be represented by a secondary host, your ISP or your software/hardware vendor. Determining those costs are necessary and requires due diligence.

The title of this chapter is "***Waiting on Mr. Murphy***" with the thought that Murphy's Law is a factor to consider. For those of you not familiar with Murphy's Law, here is the background.

"If anything can go wrong, it will"

"This phrase was born at Edwards Air Force Base in 1949 at North Base. It was named after Capt. Edward A. Murphy; an engineer working on Air Force Project MX981, designed to see how much sudden deceleration a person can stand in a crash. One day, after finding that a transducer was wired wrong, he cursed the technician responsible and said, "If there is any way to do it wrong, he'll find it." The contractor's project manager kept a list of "laws" and added this one, which he called Murphy's Law. Actually, what he did was take an old law that had been around for years in a more basic form and give it a name.

Shortly afterwards, the Air Force doctor (Dr. John Paul Stapp) who rode a sled on the deceleration track to a stop, pulling 40 Gs, gave a press conference. He said that their good safety record on the project was due to a **firm belief in Murphy's Law** and in the necessity to try and circumvent it."[1] Prepare your mind to be intellectually honest with yourself. This is a must as you consider what's important and what's not important.

---

[1]   http://www.murphys-laws.com/murphy/murphy-true.html, (October 2006)

Preparing

With the growing need for websites to service the information hungry population of the world, the Internet is becoming the first place for seeking news, entertainment, shopping and more by many people.

The ability for the average person to have their own website is well within the reach of most people. While websites can span from a simple website builder on your host to spending thousands of dollars on developers, and artists to compose a site, maintain it, and keep it fresh—somewhere in the middle falls Joomla!™.

Joomla!™ is a wonderful product that is a fully volunteer driven effort, supported by many independent coders offering up new and useful extensions to it on a regular basis. With Joomla!™ a small or medium business can have in a matter of a couple of weeks, a very professional web presence, complete with most any feature you can think of including multi-language support.

With such an easy-to-use product, more and more individuals who are not web-site administrators by training or trade have been attacked by the evil malcontents who seek to damage, destroy, and devastate web sites, servers, and more. Sometimes for fun, sometimes for evil intent. The intent of this book is to help you prevent as much damage as possible and to recover quickly in the event of an outage.

It is my belief that Joomla!™ is poised to start nibbling at the edge of the enterprise computing segments and will have a greater role in websites worldwide. Therefore it is imperative that the Joomla!™ community begin adopting enterprise level practices for site and data security maintenance.

This book will give the site admin, a basis from which to respond to outages, and to report possible new attacks, yet undiscovered, in a orderly manner that will help the community address them quickly and to receive help.

My desire is that you take this book, apply it to your sites, your businesses and your mindset. As exploits will come and get resolved, more will come.

You have to be prepared.

How this book will work for you

This is a *working book* that has been designed from my experience gained over the years working with many customers in the Fortune 100 and 1000 class companies, small to medium businesses, Federal Government, Higher Education, medical and K-12 schools.

As you proceed through this book note it is designed to provide key foundational concepts all along the way and give you a solid working knowledge of maintaining your Joomla!™ site while preparing for disaster.

You will find the following learning aids as you read through the book.

Admin focus:

This is a topic that is of great importance. Take the time to read it and understand it as it is critical to your success

Various forms:

Throughout this book you will find forms that you need to fill out as you encounter them. Don't worry about getting them exactly right. They are repeated in their entirety in the back of the book. Additionally you can visit our site at **www.joomspyder.com** to download the entire set of forms.

This book features many quotes by Sun Tzu whom you may not know. He was born around 2500 BC in China. His now famous treatise known as *The Art of War,* is required reading by American military schools, and is widely regarded in China as their manual of operations. While the title sounds barbarous the philosophy, and purpose of the book is to *win without aggression*. This can apply to the real battlefields in the world or to something as mundane as managing your website.

For me, I have studied *The Art of War* thoroughly and own many different translations. It has taught me more about strategy, and achieving objectives than ninety-nine percent of the experts on the book shelf today.

Sun Tzu advocates before engaging in any conflict or action you should ensure *you know yourself first.*

> **Know yourself; know your enemy and you will win 100 out of 100 battles**
> **Know yourself but *not* your enemy and you will win 50 and lose 50**
> **Know *neither yourself nor your* enemy and you will be defeated in every battle[2]**

You will walk away from reading this with a working plan, and a method to keep your plan fresh and alive. I advocate doing mock disasters because:

> **"No plan survives first engagement with the enemy"**
> Von Clausewitz.—Prussian Military Thinker

Testing *your plan* is no different than firemen practicing putting out fires or rescuing people from a building. You will find flaws, holes, and problems with your plan as you move through the mock drills. Do not be disheartened, as this only serves to strengthen your plan.

---

[2]   Paraphrased by author from The Art of War—http://www.gutenberg.org/etext/17405

In my career I have had the opportunity to work closely with a Fortune 100 company helping to design, and build out their disaster recovery solution. This included everything from concept, hardware, and software selection all the way to spending the next two years drilling and testing with them. They did have an opportunity to use their plan in real life twice, and it worked as it was designed, honed, and polished.

My role during the tests was that of a neutral observer of all that went on through out the regular drills. The first time the drill was conducted a large portion of the staff laughed it off, and treated it as a joke. Needless to say the test was a miserable failure. The staff during the next test was more engaged, but had not started taking it seriously yet. In fact one of the key staff members spent time playing fantasy baseball on his computer during portions of the test.

Another issue was related to a member of the staff who was in her seventh month of pregnancy. She was very uncomfortable and this was distracting to everyone who wanted to ensure her comfort. The fact that she was pregnant had not been factored in. No consideration of her *needs* in advance, or any planning for it, such as a quiet place to rest or snacks, etc., had been given. Incidentally, the same line of reasoning would apply to a physically handicapped employee. Consider your staffs physical needs, and creature comforts before testing time.

In each of these tests I reported without emotion, my findings, which included informing the CIO in detail on the staff's performance. As uncomfortable as this was it served to refine the plan.

The plan, procedures, and documentation were refined until they yielded consistent results. The last two disaster drills I observed earned them an *A+ recommendation*. The staff knew their roles, understood the documentation and was truly engaged. If disaster visits them again, they will likely come out unscathed because they are prepared for it.

Know your enemy, know yourself.

You can through a small amount of hard work, have a solid, working plan that will most likely survive an encounter with the enemy.

On the point of enemies, your website, and business has many. They come in various forms, some disguised as good things, such as upgrades. Some do not pretend to hide, but announce their presence like a dictator bent on ruling the country with an iron fist. These come in the form of those who openly attack and deface your websites

Perhaps your enemy is simply lack of knowledge, the weather, a power outage or hardware failure. Your enemy is alive, well, and is planning to attack you; even if that enemy has not any conscious thought, such as code, that has an undiscovered flaw.

You must prepare and be ready.

Yet in each engagement with the enemy is a gift if you are wise enough to see it, and take advantage of it, you will reap the benefits.

> *Every adversity, every failure, every heartache carries with it the seed*
> *of an equal or greater benefit.*[3]

Napoleon Hill—Think and grow rich

---

[3]   http://www.quoteopia.com/famous.php?quotesby=napoleonhill (Dec. 2006)

Each time you face a *crisis* or a *disaster* you have the opportunity to improve your defenses, increase your knowledge and update your plan. Sharing with the Joomla!™ community increases the overall knowledge available. Trouble and problems will come, no doubt, but take full advantage of it to improve.

Be prepared by being knowledgeable of your self and of your enemy.

Defining disaster levels

If you are running a family photo site or a warm, and friendly blog site, and it is strictly a, hobby this book will have little meaning to you. However if you are running say an ecommerce business, the guide you create from this should be your constant companion.

In any risk determination, you need to decide on the criticality, to your business the portions of your site that would be most devastated should they become damaged, and develop a plan around that. While everyone defines disasters by a differently I have defined them as follows.

Level—1—In this scenario your *core operations are shut down*. Your employees and customers cannot work for what ever reason.

Level—2—Your site is up but large portions of it are *experiencing an outage*, either through something out of the ordinary like an incorrectly configured DNS, a portion of the Internet failing or distributed denial of service (dDoS) attacks. In this scenario, your employees and customers may have partial access to your site.

Level—3—is defined as a *working failure*. Part of your site is down but it does not stop critical operations such as order entry. There is little to no impact to your operations.

Level—4—*Non-critical* or in other words, if your statistics package is not working, you are possibly upset, but by no means down or non-operational.

Question yourself against these scenarios. If you are running an e-commerce site, which scenario would it be? *Most likely Scenario 1.*

Your personal blog site clearly in most cases would fall into Level 4.

This is an introductory view and you will not need to reference this again.

What is risk tolerance?

When a disaster happens, without proper training, documentation or processes, human nature is to panic.

In any disaster you must approach it with a non-panicked mind as this is the wrong time to lose your head and start pushing buttons.

Risk

First things first, are assessing the level of *risk* your website can tolerate. Using the example of the United States 911 emergency phone system as an analog, the emergency system (911) has nearly (in practical terms) *zero tolerance* for downtime. A personal blog has 100 percent tolerance for risk.

Assess your risk in this manner to determine the risk versus the reward of building a plan

Low to no risk ←————————————————————————→ **High, Life threatening Risk**
    [blog site]   **[e-commerce]**   **[911 emergency system]**

Where on this scale does your site live?

This example is not meant to imply priority. The purpose is to introduce you to an idea of how much risk that can be tolerated based on the purpose of the site. If your blog is mission critical then it would go much farther on the scale to the right.

Ask your self "Can you tolerate downtime?" and if so, how much?

Asking the hard questions helps you determine the real truth. Can you stand two days down without financial impact or harm? If yes, then ask, can you stand three, four or even five?

Disaster Preparedness

Data protection is the core tenet of a disaster preparedness effort. Many disaster preparedness plans include having a backup site where operations can continue uninterrupted, known as a failover site. The idea of having a failover site is well and good but your philosophy should be doing everything in your power to protect your data locally then extending *that plan* geographically, [such as having a failover site]. In this case *local* refers to where your site is hosted.

The susceptibility and survivability of your local data is the most important factor. In your planning efforts you need to examine your backup, and recovery processes. After all a restoration is only as good as the last good backup. Establishing solid procedures, and policies locally, extending those to another site is the preferred method for recovery.

When talking to customers in the information technology world, if the subject of disaster preparedness would come up I would ask, "What is your strategy in the event you had a very severe outage?" The answer usually was, "we have backup tapes and we would restore them." That's great I would think and ask "When was the last time you tested restoring them?" More often than not the answer was "we don't know."

Factors of disaster preparedness to consider:

- What will the plan cost? This many times can be a show stopper for a plan because it is not usually well known, and unless the costs can be justified no one will spend the time, effort, or money to do it.
- Does your insurance cover hardware replacement?
- Can you obtain new hardware and install it in a timely fashion?
- If you are on a shared host is there a charge to restore?
- How much *data loss (measured as some point time)* known as *recovery point objective* (**RPO**) can you stand?
- How much downtime (measured in minutes, hours, days) known as the *recovery time objective* (**RPO**) can you stand? This is also known as the time between the failure and system restoration.
- The recovery time objective (**RTO**) includes stopping what you're doing, getting everything healthy—or as in the case of an attack—getting rid of the attacker and attacked parts.

Restoring the data, and getting systems back online as soon as possible are your top priorities. Should you wish to explore these topics, and others in greater detail than is touched on here I recommend the following books.

Business Continuity and Disaster Recovery for InfoSec Managers
By PhD, CISM, John Rittinghouse and PhD, CISM, CISSP, James F. Ransome

Disaster Recovery planning—preparing for the unthinkable.
Jon William Toigo

Failure response—what do you do now?

If you observed a car accident you would most likely call the police, or medical personal to respond to it. When dialing 911, (in the USA), you are connected immediately to the first responders who will gather the information, and dispatch the appropriate emergency personal.

If you were to accidentally ingest poison you would call the poison control hotline where you would receive specific instructions on the antidote for the poison consumed. Both of these groups are trained to respond, and follow *strict processes* to protect, and save human life, and property.

Your success in responding to a failure, attack or disaster is based in strict processes as well. You need to have defined set processes regarding how you will respond, and what direction you will take to regain a healthy, working site as quickly as possible.

Basic steps to take when an outage occurs:

- Realize there is an outage.
- Making a determination of the root cause of the outage.
- Initiating your disaster plan to regain control, and bring your site back online.
- Communications about the disaster should be directed to all parties including to the stakeholders, employees, and where appropriate the general public as to the reason for the outage.
- Reviewing the (post-mortem) disaster to determine where the flaws in your system are, and shore them up through the improvement of the processes.

Can you afford NOT to have a disaster preparedness plan?

This evokes "Of course!" when asked of the uninitiated. The question seems elementary but it is related to how serious you are about maintaining your site, and having as little downtime as possible. It must be asked to have an open and intellectual dialog about your business.

Depending on your particular uptime objectives your plan could cost a lot or a little.

Consider the following items about costs:

- If the amount of down time will not result in significant financial loss then clearly any large sums of money spent on DR will be a waste.
- On the opposite end of the scale if you stand to lose significant revenue when your site is down then spending the money is very justified.

You, as the site admin, business owner or the stakeholder in your future have to make that judgment call.

Assessing the risk to your organization

Open source often draws fire from the critics in the commercial world in that *it's open, everyone can see the code*. Yes, it is somewhat true, crackers, and evil-doers have complete access, and do have an advantage of seeing the code to find holes. However this doesn't mean you are safe using commercial software as any news story of recent years will attest too. You cannot see the commercial software code, yet you may be at risk as well. Keeping your system patched, your permissions correct and a few other simple items can keep you very safe.

A simple cursory read on the Joomla!™ forums shows that first thing many people do is panic. And in the words of the wonderful fictional world of *The Hitchhikers Guide to the Galaxy that states in large, friendly letters,* **Don't Panic.**[4]

People generally panic when they do not have a plan. Think about times that you were admitted to an emergency room, you might have been panicky due to a heart attack, birth, injury or the like. I doubt you noticed the lack of panic on the part of the staff. They remained calm, asking for your information, how you feel, your name, etc. They calmly took your vitals, while reassuring you they were going to take care of you.

In the event of a bona-fide life threatening emergency, they react with great speed, but no panic. They realize the time-sensitive nature of stabilizing a person who is badly injured and needs immediate life sustaining help. Still they do not crumble into a ball, grab the medical text book, and start reading to determine what next steps to take.

Medical professionals depend on a system of processes, and training to manage rather than react to the emergency. One story I read recently was about a pioneer in heart care. He put together a system of diagnosis for emergency rooms to make a very quick, and highly accurate determination of a true cardiac event versus heartburn from eating bad food. Many lives were saved that may have been lost due to misdiagnosis through this breakthrough method.

What does this have to do you and your site? Like the doctor you need to diagnose a "true" outage VS a temporary hiccup with your ISP and responding accordingly in a timely fashion.

To do so you need a strategic written plan, complete with tactical objectives of getting your site running as quickly as you can—no matter what the reason for the interruption.

---

4   Adams, Douglas, "The Hitchhikers Guide to the Galaxy", (Harmony Books, New York, 1979), 27

Admin focus: What are you trying to protect

You must define what you're trying to protect.

Examples include
Customer data, credit card, purchasing information, Medical information,
private (confidential) data that you may be dealing with.

- Is my site an ecommerce store?
- Does it store personal customer information?
- How sensitive is the data on my site if it got into the wild?
- If it were medical or financial what would be the impact? Is mine that sensitive?

Defining this will help you to plan your disaster response

- **What are my associated costs of downtime?**

Once again you need to have a good understanding of your risk. For instance if you were shut down to the point that you couldn't recover for what ever reason, would you be obligated to continue to pay for shared hosting? If you are attacked and made into a 'spam-bot' and this drives up a huge bandwidth bill, will you be required to pay it? These are costs that are often not considered until it's too late.

- **Answer—in most cases is YES**.

Other costs to consider are replacing equipment due to fire, flood, employee theft or destruction. Do you have insurance on those items? If so have you reviewed the policy to see if it provides adequate protection?

- **Who are my stake holders?**

This is for sure yourself, your employees and your customers. It can include others on a case by case basis.

Ask yourself—who does my site having downtime affect? Who would be *impacted* by downtime of your systems? This is known as your downstream customers.

Admin focus: What are you trying to protect—continued

- **Would I be legally exposed if I my site were compromised? (For any reason).**

As an example in California the privacy laws are written to protect the consumer. Breach of personal information comes with a severe financial penalty. I strongly encourage you to speak to your legal counsel on this topic. This is not something often considered as a side effect of a disaster.

<u>**This book does not address legal issues of any sort.**</u>
<u>**I am not an attorney and I am not offering any legal advice.**</u>

You should seek out your attorney or legal council for the right answers for you. I only raise this to make you aware of it and take time to research it.

- **How long would it take you to bring your site up to working order again?**

Each site is different and there is not a single answer. If it is merely defacement, then replacing the damaged files takes only minutes. Consider though if the defacer left something, such as a *backdoor*, or *trojan horse* behind, what would the long term impact be? Until you verify for yourself that defacement was not a diversion to put something there, then you do not have an accurate time assessment. If there is a *trojan horse*, left behind then a full site restoration from a clean backup is in order. Suddenly the few minutes of time you thought it would take have morphed into a few hours. Consider this in your planning process as you look at critical systems.

Ask yourself: Who should be involved in the recovery?

- Do you conduct your backup?
- Do you have a staff member who handles backups?
- If a staff member is responsible and they leave for vacation, is there a backup employee assigned to handle the tasks?
- Is the documentation location available?
- Does your hosting company?
- If your hosting company does the backup how do you initiate a recovery?

If you have a plan already in place have you tested it?
If you have backups have you verified they will restore?

*<u>**"Trust but verify"**</u>—**President Ronald Reagan**

Closing Words

This chapter has offered you a glimpse of disaster preparedness planning.

I advocate no matter what the size of your business, a solid disaster preparedness plan is in order. As you exit this chapter keep in mind how the types of disasters could impact you, should your site encounter them.

In the exercise of thinking through scenarios consider the data that needs protection, what costs or budget can you afford versus what the worth is to your business.

Take full advantage of this book by making it work for you.

Remember dodging the bullets is a full time job.

Topics covered in this chapter

- **You have an idea of your risk tolerance**
- **Learned the value of having a disaster preparation plan**
- **Received a basic failure response concept and how you should respond to an outage.**

Chapter 2

Preparing For Battle

Getting your site fortified

Why read this chapter

This chapter discusses the basics of security for your site.

It's not a matter of if you will be attacked, but when.

Learning goals in this chapter

- Getting your site to a solid base-line security standard
- Learn to make a full backup of your system
- Identifying and removing any "AT-RISK" or easy to crack extensions from your Joomla!™-based site
- Learn how to join in the joomla.org notification forum to stay current on issues

> *Learn from history of successful battles.*
> *First you should control the situation not try to win.*
> *If you adjust to the enemy, you will find a way to win.*
> *The opportunity to win does not come from yourself.*
> *The opportunity to win comes from your enemy.*
>
> *Sun Tzu—The Art of War*

War is in progress on the Internet with the goal of destroying your website in mind. The evil-doers out there often times are trying to take over your site for purposes such as turning it into a spambot. Others may want to simply deface or destroy your site. My views of those who attack websites are no different than a person who breaks into your home; it is as deplorable. It should be dealt with swiftly, and with strong punishment.

At this point I assume you have installed Joomla!™ and are enjoying the riches of the free extensions. In those treasures, however lies a dark side; often untested thoroughly, sometimes sloppily written code that has been abandoned to rot. Code sporting known open issues that the enemy can attack. Code that should not have any negative impact on your site, if you follow good practices to maintain your site.

Case in point, a series of attacks on Joomla!™-based websites came through a few well known exploits. This is not to cast aspersions on the core team or the 3rd party developers. Rather to wake you, the administrators of your site, to the fact that in most of the cases these attacks were one-hundred percent preventable. The exploits came through unpatched third party components, older core code, and incorrect permissions among other things.

If the administrators of the exploited sites had exercised good security practices code they would have prevented or mitigated many of the attacks against their websites. These practices include such things as patching, backup, and recovery methods as well as updating of third-party extensions, and the core code.

The battle is here, whether you wish it to be or not, **you must prepare.**

Dr. W. Edward Deming is considered the father of modern Quality. In Japan the highest award is the Deming Award, it is given to those who demonstrate, consistent quality processes and an excellent product. Dr. Deming in his book ***Out of the Crisis*** lined out fourteen points of quality and seven deadly diseases that tend to infect companies universally.

Dr. Deming's fifth point

"Improve Constantly and Forever the System of Production and Service."[1]

He states "Improvement is not a one-time effort. Management is obligated to improve continually." Quality, Dr. Deming says, "must be built in at the design stage." and "teamwork is essential to the process." [1]

The meaning for us, the admins of our sites, is that we cannot launch the site and forget, going merrily about our way thinking all is well. We have to constantly improve our processes. Constantly improve our service. Constantly strive for higher uptime. I think that the idea of disaster preparedness is very well covered in the following statement from Dr. Deming.

"Putting out fires is not improvement. Finding a point of control, finding the special cause and removing it, is only putting the process back to where it was in the first place. It is not improvement of the process. [Dr. Deming attributes this conclusion to Dr. Joseph M. Juran, many years ago.] You are in a hotel. You hear someone yell fire. He runs for the fire extinguisher and pulls the alarm to call the fire department. We all get out. Extinguishing the fire does not improve the hotel.—That is not improvement of quality. That is putting out fires." [1]

What Dr. Deming is stating to us is that responding to attacks, fixing the damage is no different than the hotel fire. It does not improve the quality of your site. It puts the site back to the original state it was in pre-attack. This chapter seeks to improve the quality of your site. We explore items that are problem sources, implement improvements to your site, and move you closer to the disaster preparedness plan. In other words, we are not simply putting out fires.

Quality steps to fortify your site

Here are some important steps needed to form the basis of security on your site.

1. Proper system wide settings: Verifying the minimum safe levels needed
2. Settings and verifications of versions: Setting of variables such as Global registers, safe mode and certain PHP server settings
3. Remove any code that is considered "at-risk." This can include code that is known to have open issues or code found to be unreliable.
4. Using .htaccess to mitigate attacks to your site
5. Permissions: Checking to see that you have files and directories set correctly
6. Upgrading your core version. Many sites are potentially still running older core code.
7. Updating to the latest safe level is mandatory for secure operations

---

[1]   Walton, Mary, "*The Deming Management Method*" (Chicago: Perigee Books, 1986), 66–67.

Step 1—Proper system settings

You will rest better knowing you have a solid baseline from which to build your site upon. Much like a home with a bad foundation the walls and roof will crack letting in all kinds of bad things. If a strong wind comes it could topple the house.

Your website must have a solid foundation to rest upon to protect you against not only those seeking to destroy you but Mr. Murphy himself. In this section we explore the concepts necessary to establishing a solid baseline, remove common flaws, and get you ready for bigger things.

First thing please login to your administrative console.

Click on System → System Info
Examine these settings:

***The two important one's you want to make sure
are set are underlined.***

Safe Mode:	**OFF**
Open basedir:	none
Display Errors:	ON
Short Open Tags:	ON
File Uploads:	ON
Magic Quotes:	ON
Register Globals:	**OFF**
Output Buffering:	OFF
Session save path:	/tmp
Session auto start:	0
XML enabled:	Yes
Zlib enabled:	Yes
Disabled Functions:	none
WYSIWYG Editor: No WYSIWYG Editor	

Another easy method to check your site settings is this short PHP code snippet that will give you the server's entire variables, settings and versions running.

```
<?php phpinfo();?>
```

This will provide you a comprehensive report on your server.

Step 2—Settings and verification of versions

Steps to set the REGISTER GLOBALS = ON to REGISTER GLOBALS = OFF

Method 1:

Contact your hosting provider and ask them to switch register_globals to OFF.

Method 2:

If your host will not turn this setting to OFF try these settings in globals.php

define('RG_EMULATION', 0)

(Currently this is true but is subject to change).

Note: This only works if you run on an Apache server and PHP is installed as an Apache module

Other information can be found at this URL:

http://forum.joomla.org/index.php/topic,32714.0.html for more information on this.

Turn off safe mode:

If you are unable to turn off SAFE MODE contact your host and request the change.

Minimum safe Joomla!™ version
As of this writing, the CORE Joomla!™ is 1.0.12. You should be at the minimum of 1.0.11. Login to your administrative console and scroll all the way down you should see this:

Joomla! is Free Software released under the GNU/GPL License.
Joomla! 1.0.11 Stable [Sunbow] 28 August 2006 20:00 UTC
Check for latest Version

If you see any thing LESS than the above version you *are at risk*.

Please note that by the time this book reaches your hands there may be a greater version available. This represents the safest minimum at the time.

Visit www.joomla.org and download the most current set of patches to get you to a minimum of 1.0.12.

Step 3—Remove any at risk code

If at this point you have not been compromised, you should ensure that you do not have any *at-risk* code. For a complete listing of current *at risk* extensions please visit the following link on the forum:

http://forum.joomla.org/index.php/topic,79477.0.html

ACTION: Visit the above link and subscribe today

Here you will find a list of extensions that are known to have security flaws.

Next step is to subscribe to the security announcements:

http://forum.joomla.org/index.php?action=notifyboard;board=8.0

ACTION: Visit the above link and subscribe today

Look to your lower left and click YES I WANT TO BE NOTIFIED. This will keep you up to date on important security alerts and news that is relevant to securing your site.

If you do not have a login ID you need to create on first.

After subscribing to this forum posting, please review your site for any possible issues that you may have missed.

.HTACCESS

Using .htaccess to protect your site

This chapter *is not* a comprehensive review or tutorial on *.htaccess*. We will show you a few basic items to give you an idea of its power. While doing so you will learn specific settings to improve the security of your site.

The .htaccess file is a text file that is specifically designed to make changes on a *per directory basis*. This file can contain one, two, or as many instructions as you like that tell the server how to handle a directory in a certain way.

The .htaccess file impacts the *directory* it resides in and all the subdirectories below it. This means that you can insert .htaccess files at lower or deeper levels in your file structure for fine-grained control.

For example using *.htaccess* to prevent visitors from viewing a particular directory is simple. Let's say you have a directory called/**manuals**. In that directory you have a set of e-books you want to protect from prying eyes. Place in your/**manuals** directory a .htaccess file with the command below in it to keep the directory from being listed or browsed.

IndexIgnore[2]

Other uses include password protecting directories, controlling access, stopping kiddie scripts and more.

For the purposes of this book we will only discuss *.htaccess* at the root level of the site.

---

[2]   Note this only works with Apache web server

What is .htaccess?

.htaccess files [are *distributed configuration files* and they] provide a way to make configuration changes on a per-directory basis. A file containing one or more configuration directives is placed in a particular directory, and the directives apply to that directory, and all subdirectories thereof.[3]

As a site admin you should have a working knowledge of this powerful solution to some bad problems. For example to create a custom redirection for an error pages you could use this:

Customize your error messages
ErrorDocument 403/verboten.html
ErrorDocument 404/nothere.html
ErrorDocument 500/serverblewup.html

Many common exploits can be stopped with a well written .htaccess file. Additionally if there are 'evil-doers' afoot who are attempting to attack your site, you can block the offending inbound IP address.

There are lots of reasons to use an .htaccess file, yet the most important one I want you to take away is the fact that a well written, and deployed, .htaccess file can be a great tool to stop exploits.

**Note: Setting the permissions on the .htaccess file to 644
allows it to be used by server but prevents viewing through the browser.**

For more information about using .htaccess please
visit this well written online guide:

http://www.javascriptkit.com/howto/htaccess.shtml

If you are unsure how to write a good .htaccess command visit:

http://cooletips.de/htaccess/

---

[3]   http://httpd.apache.org/docs/2.2/howto/htaccess.html (accessed: October 2006)

Step 4—Using .htaccess to mitigate exploits

The following added to the .htaccess file should mitigate many common exploits:

Steps:
1. Rename htaccess.txt to .htaccess in your ROOT directory (if you have not already done so)
2. Open for editing and add the following lines to the END of the file, SAVE and CLOSE.

```
########## Begin—Rewrite rules to block out some common exploits
#
# Block out any script trying to set a mosConfig value through the URL
RewriteCond %{QUERY_STRING} mosConfig_[a-zA-Z_]{1,21}(=|\%3D) [OR]
# Block out any script trying to base64_encode crap to send via URL
RewriteCond %{QUERY_STRING} base64_encode.*\(.*\) [OR]
# Block out any script that includes a <script> tag in URL
RewriteCond %{QUERY_STRING} (\<|%3C).*script.*(\>|%3E) [NC,OR]
# Block out any script trying to set a PHP GLOBALS variable via URL
RewriteCond %{QUERY_STRING} GLOBALS(=|\[|\%[0–9A-Z]{0,2}) [OR]
# Block out any script trying to modify a _REQUEST variable via URL
RewriteCond %{QUERY_STRING} _REQUEST(=|\[|\%[0–9A-Z]{0,2})
# Send all blocked request to homepage with 403 Forbidden error!
RewriteRule ^(.*)$ index.php [F,L]
#
########## End—Rewrite rules to block out some common exploits
```
Source: Joomla!™ Forums

Disclaimer: Be SURE and read
http://forum.joomla.org/index.php/topic,75376.0.html and

http://forum.joomla.org/index.php/topic,76578.msg388696.html#msg388696
in the security forums of Joomla.org BEFORE YOU add this to your
site for the latest information.

And TEST your site thoroughly to ensure your unique configuration works with this.
This code is currently working on several sites without problems.
There is no guarantee that this will stop any exploits. Use at your own risk.

These steps should not have any impact on your shared hosting site. However before you make any changes
always consult your hosting provider first.

Remember: ALWAYS make a FULL backup of everything before beginning.

Permissions and Joomla!™

Understanding permissions

In any UNIX system, or other operating systems, such as Linux, FreeBSD, Debian, etc., the topic of permissions has been beat to little pieces, in books, and online publications. Yet I find this topic needs to be covered to have a complete understanding to help stop exploits. When permissions get screwed up, the entire system is out of whack. To understand permissions, let me use an analogy of your home; **your home = your site**. You represent the "Owner", your family members represent "Group", and the general public represents "Others", or the public at large.

When we assign permissions we use a numbering system known as *Octal.*[4]

You the *Owner* have full run of every room and feature of your home. In octal this would be represented as 7 octal (4+2+1 in octal).

However, your kids do not have *permission* to the master bedroom of the house yet they do have full permission of the living room, bathroom and their bedrooms. They are represented as ***Group***. In octal this level of permission would be 6 octal or (4+2+0 in octal).

If someone comes and knocks on your door, you can give them *permission* to come in and use what ever portion of the home you see fit. You have the *right* to eject them from your home or not even let them in. You decide on the *Rights* you grant.

Now let's say that John Q. Public is really John. Q. Evil—He's a thief and a malcontent, you leave your door unlocked, and he comes in finding all the other *doors* in the house unlocked (*owner, group, other all set to octal 7 represented by 777*). He finds your valuables lying out in the open in your bedroom and he takes them (think of this as stealing your customer data from your site). Maybe he is an artist and sprays your walls with fuchsia spray paint to show his artistic side (this could be a defacement of your site). Maybe he slips in hiding a tiny web cam to watch you and steal your personal life; this is akin to putting a Trojan horse on your site.

If your site were your home you would lock the outside door represented in octal as (755 or 644) giving the thief permission to view your house from the outside and maybe even knock on the door. The interior of your home remains safe. In your bedroom you have your valuables laying on the dresser, however John Q. Evil cannot see them or touch them as he does not have permission to enter.

Your kids come home (Group), they have full permission to parts of the house, they unlock the door, come in and plop down to watch TV (Execute).

However they aren't allowed to watch TV in your bedroom (hence NO X or *execute* bit on the resource known as your master bedroom). They belong to the *Group* who has house wide permissions to most of the house but not all the house.

In our example of your home and your family, the users can be represented by guests in your home, possibly your children or yourself.

The owner is represented *solely* as you, the home owner. In this home example, your children have possessions that belong to them. In essence at their level they are the *owner of their space* and have limited power to dictate who can do what with their possessions. They are below the *root* level of the Home Owner, that being you,

---

4   For a better understanding of octal see the upcoming **Admin Focus:** *What is Octal*.

hence they could ask for permission to paint their room yellow and you as the *owner* could grant them that *right* to paint their room but no other room in the house.

What this represents is a file structure hierarchy, where each part of the house and its contents could be thought of as files, resources, subdirectories and the like. The *home* itself represents the actual main root directory of the website. In essence *this house is* the website.

You the homeowner operate like the root or admin of the site at that topmost level, allowing permissions to flow down from you. Permissions cannot be granted to anyone else below you our outside the home without your knowledge.

Setting all the files and subdirectories on your site to 777 for instance would be the same as placing a large ad in the paper or putting up a sign saying, "my house is open and you are free to roam through and do exactly as you please including setting it on fire and burning it down."

Clearly this is not something you would do and the example is taken to the ridiculous to make a point.

In the next pages we take this concept and learn more using real life examples and terms to apply proper permissions to our website.

Admin Focus—What is OCTAL? [3]

The octal numeral system is the base-8 number system, and uses the digits 0 to 7.

Octal numerals can be made from binary numerals by grouping consecutive digits into groups of three (starting from the right). For example, the binary representation for decimal 74 is 1001010, which groups into 1 001 010—so the octal representation is 112.

We count the same as in decimal however with eight digits instead of ten. This results in changing the digits to the left more frequently.

When you count in base 8, you get:

```
  0   1   2   3   4   5   6   7
 10  11  12  13  14  15  16  17
 20  21  22  23  24  25  26  27
              ...
 70  71  72  73  74  75  76  77
100 101 102 103 104 105 106 107
110 111 112 113 114 115 116 117
              ...
170 171 172 173 174 175 176 177
200 201 202 203 204 205 206 207
210 212 212 213 214 215 216 217
              ...
270 271 272 273 274 275 276 277
300 301 302 303 304 305 306 307
310 312 312 313 314 315 316 317
```

You will note the octal number 10 follows 7, thus 10 in octal is like saying 8 in decimal. The rest of the numbers follow suite.

Permissions and your site

UNIX was developed in a world where security was not as much of a consideration as it might have been had the developers of been able to see the future. Yet much work has been done to add security measures to protect computers, data, sites, etc.

One of these added security features is known as *permissions.*

Permissions are a set of rules that govern who gets permission to see, use and change files.

Many common exploits on sites are the result of incorrectly set permissions.

This book will not address the details of setting OS permissions on your host, it explores in detail what permissions are, how to understand them, and what the proper settings should be for your website.

Permissions at their most base or atomic level are described by three letters.

Those letters are:

R for read
W for Write
X for Execute

Permissions are assigned on a *category* level. There are four categories known as:

D for Directory
O for Owner
G for group
P for public (often this is the outside world)

Each of these has three (3) *bits* that can be turned on or turned off accordingly to set a specific permission level. Each group can have Read, Write and Execute privileges. Setting these incorrectly can result in letting the wrong people in.

The bits are represented by a numbering system known as *octal.* Octal is represented by the numbers 0–7 and is known as *base-8.* For comparison, the numbering system we use in everyday life is known as *base-10 using* the numbers 0–9.

Each *bit* represents a permission level, defined in such as way that if you select them you have an octal representation, of the permissions.

Understanding permissions

Who does the OS consider a USER?

Users on a *nix (Linux, UNIX, etc.) operating system are a logical representation of the real person or a *machine process*. Each user receives an *id* that in turn is allowed *to do* something within the system. Many attacks can be avoided if the permissions of *who is allowed* and *who is not allowed* are set correctly.

Organizing users by *Groups*

Each *user* can belong to one or many *groups*. We control access to all parts of the system by identifying the permissions a *group* has and then assigning *users* into that *group*. That way if you want to add a new *user* to a *group* you do not have to go and assign each right and privilege to that *user*. They take on the rights of the *group*.

Who owns what?

This is an easy place to trip up; for instance if you set all the permissions across all *files* and *directories* to 777 you have just said that *everyone* has rights to read, write and execute every file.

To understand, this consider that in any Unix based operating system or derivative the system is *file* based, that is every thing is treated as if it were a *file*. Hence every file must have an *owner* and a *group* who owns it, and *permissions* to access it.

- Each file can be owned by a *user*
- That *user* can be a member of a *group* that *owns* that file
- A *user* can be a user on the system, but be restricted from *group* or a *file*. Such as say the password file which is restricted information.

Permissions

There are three permission levels for each file in a *nix system. Each of the *bits* correlates to *owner* (of the file), *group* and *public* access to the file or *directory*.

These bits say I can

* read it
* write it (*change the file*)
* execute it (*or run it*)

Understanding permissions on *nix systems

Did you know that *directories* have permissions too? In fact the *group* and *public* members can tamper with your **directory structure** *if* your permissions are set to, 7 into the **d** position. This means anyone can do anything to my directories and files. Or in other words this essentially means that a user with write access to a directory can delete files in the directory. This setting overrides individual file settings. Be certain before you grant WRITE access to any file outside of owner.

How do we change the files?

There are two methods to do so. One is if you have access to the console of your server you can use the CHMOD to alter permissions or use your favorite FTP client. For the purposes of our discussion and this book we'll stick to FTP CHMOD or in other words, using your FTP programs to tell it to change files.

Bits, bits, bits 4=r (read) 2=w (write) 1=x (execute)

These numbers are **OCTAL** representations, but can be added like base 10 numbers. To give an owner FULL permissions to a file set the bits to 777 (RXW) or in other words 4+2+1=7 in the appropriate section.

To give the same file only read and execute you would add 4 (read) + 0 (not allowed to write) + 1 (allowed to execute) which equals 5. You would continue to do the same for the WORLD or others. This would be read as 755

What the OWNER can do (first bit)
What the GROUP who owns it can do (second bit)
What PUBLIC or everyone can do (third bit)

For any given ownership relation, we use three bits to specify access permissions: the first to denote read (r) access, the second to denote write (w) access and the third to denote execute (x) access. What this means is that the owner can do anything with the file, but group owners and the rest of the world can only read or execute it.

Remember permissions flow down from the top.

Understanding permissions on *nix systems

Starting at the second to the left bit you see it has a pattern of RWX—this means the OWNER (in this case the admin) can read, write and execute the directory and it's files. Granting them the authority to do what he or she wishes.

The second set of three bits reads—. This says that the GROUP cannot READ, WRITE or EXECUTE the contents. This prevents the file from being overwritten The third set of three bits reads R-X. This is PUBLIC or anyone coming into our site. They can in this example READ the contents, and execute but cannot change it by overwriting it or modifying it.

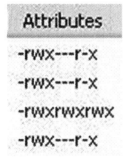

Step 5—Setting correct permissions

ACTION REQUIRED: Open your FTP program to check your permissions on your files and directories. Your files and directories should be set to:

Directories: 755
Files in the directories to: 644
For all the files in the *root* of your site set them to: 644

This is an IMPORTANT step for complete site hardening

It is noteworthy to point out that you as the administrator may have a need to change permissions differently, but in most cases these should be the default for your sites. If you have a need for setting something to 777 consider using a combination of the .htaccess commands, and permissions to setup a scenario where you will not leave an open hole.

Admin Focus: Ensuring your 3rd party extensions are safe

During the writing of this book attacks were launched against several Joomla!™-based sites. Depending on the degree of the attack, sites were either completely comprised or suffered defacements.

The suspect components that allowed the attacks to happen will most likely be fixed or removed by the time this book comes to you. However for historical and possible future implications I want to cover some details and the fix.

For our purposes I'll refer to Ext_Calendar, as the developer had stopped work on it according to the Joomla!™ forum about two years ago. Certain portions of this component were being called from outside Joomla!™ and allowed to execute directly. Attackers were able exploit this fact through the component as it was missing vital code to prevent just such an attack. This allowed the attackers to walk right through doing what ever they pleased.

Additionally there are several PERL script attacks floating around and usually these scripts and others like them are downloaded into the servers/tmp directory, the cache or media directories. After they execute they will often times delete themselves to cover their tracks. Removal of these is your highest priority to prevent your site participating in a DDoS (distributed denial of service attack).

If you are running any 3rd party components, modules, mambots or Plugins you must check for this line. This line should appear as the first line of CODE after the **"<?php"**

Code snip: ('_VALID_MOS') or die('Restricted access');

It is imperative that you check files with the extension "*.php.*" To do this, open the file with your FTP editor or locally on your workstation using a text editor.

You can quickly review each of the files for it.

Step 6—Upgrading your Joomla!™

At this point you are ready to upgrade your Joomla!™ to v1.0.12

This example only applies to Joomla!™ that released before version 1.5. At the time of writing 1.0.12 was the standard. Please visit the Joomla!™ forums for the latest information OR visit www.joomspyder.com for updates to this book.

Steps to upgrade your base Joomla!™ code:

Visit the **www.joomla.org** site for the latest information on any security patches, upgrade procedures, or news.

Upgrading from any version of Joomla!™ 1.0.x to 1.0.12, simply involves overwriting your current sites files, with the files in the proper patch package that applies to your site.

e.g., If you are running Joomla!™ 1.0.5, you will need the 1.0.5 to 1.0.12 Patch Package.

This is done by uncompressing the patch package, then using an FTP client to transfer these files to your server and overwrite the existing files. Common problems include files that did not transfer properly, and are characterized by any number of odd or hard to diagnosis errors.

Many hosts will provide a web based administration tool such as CPanel or Plesk. You can use these to upload the patch package to your server

Next make a list of the 3rd party extensions you are running and check on the Joomla!™ site to ensure you have the latest versions.

After you do all these steps **run another FULL backup** including the files, directories, and database dump.

BE SURE YOU HAVE MADE A *FULL* BACKUP BEFORE ANY UPGRADES.

Special note: These upgrade procedures will most likely not apply to version 1.5.
Please consult the support forums for more information

Admin Focus: Third party components with security holes and their effect.

Details of a hacked website

Version of Joomla!™ **1.0.10**
Components: DOCMan v1.3 RC2, ExtCalendar 2, SMF bridge 1.5
PHP version.4.2
MySql version .1.19-standard
Apache version.3.34 (Unix)

This site, while running 1.0.10 was compromised through ExtCalendar 2

<u>In this case the admin was truly caught unaware through the fault of ExtCalendar.</u>

Ext_Cal had at the time of writing a known security flaw allowing the crackers to reach in and damage sites. If this site were on shared hosting, they could potentially drive through damaging other sites hosted on the same physical machines.

That is why it is important to keep up to date on exploits.

For instance: searching on the site: www.frsirt.com for ExtCalendar would reveal:

ExtCalendar Module for Mambo "mosConfig_absolute_path" File Inclusion Vulnerability

*The admin in all fairness would not have had time to respond most likely. The point of this case study is to show you that the 'bad-guys' watch for these exploits to be revealed and **IMMEDIATELY** use them to attack your sites.*

Advisory ID: FrSIRT/ADV-2006–2711 CVE ID: GENERIC-MAP-NO-MATCH

Technical Description

A vulnerability has been identified in ExtCalendar (module for Mambo), which may be exploited by attackers to execute arbitrary commands. This flaw is due to an input validation error in the "extcalendar.php" script that fails to validate the "mosConfig_absolute_path" parameter, which could be exploited by remote attackers to include malicious files and execute arbitrary commands with the privileges of the web server.

Source: www.frsirt.com

This advisory was made public and the attack hit within a short time after.

Passwords

Not all passwords are created equal and they [***passwords***] deserve more attention than we usually give them—both in their conception and handling thereafter. Passwords have become so common, so much part of our daily lives that we treat our passwords with little care or regard for their protection. We come up with weak passwords that are easy to guess, storing them unprotected on our desktops. We write them down, on little sticky notes attached to our computer screens for the world to see.

Creating a *good* and *strong* password

It is tempting to use your birth date as your password, or your dog's name, or even the street where you live. These types of passwords are as obvious to crackers as they are to you. The challenge in creating a cracker-proof password is to make the password difficult to guess without making it impossible for you to remember. To create and maintain strong passwords, start with these suggestions.

- Use a combination of uppercase, lowercase letters, symbols, and numbers.
- Make sure your passwords are at least eight characters long.
- The more characters your passwords contain, the more difficult they are to guess.
- Try to make your passwords as meaningless and random as possible.
- Use different passwords for each account.
- Change your passwords regularly.
- Set a date in your day planner or online calendar to prompt you to change your password
- Never write your passwords down and never give them out—to anyone.
- Never use your name or any numbers associated with you, as in your birth date, nickname, age, height or weight.
- Don't use your user or login name in any form you fill out—you do not know who has access to those forms.
- No pet names or family member names
- Avoid using a solitary word in any language due to "dictionary" attacks
- Never use "password" or "Passcode" as your password. *This is a common problem.*
- Do not use any personal information, including license plate numbers, telephone numbers, social security numbers, your automobile's make or model, where you live, etc.
- Never store your passwords on your computer.

Passwords

If you use this technique, mixing in a few numbers, and/or symbols increases the complexity of the password, making it more secure. Another approach is to take two short words with nothing in common and combine them with punctuation or numerals. Always remember to use both uppercase and lowercase letters.

Never use obvious or common words with vowels replaced by symbols or numbers because this is one of the common techniques a cracker will try.

Keep in mind that the password you choose is one that will allow you into your site. Should this password be compromised, your site could be compromised.

One suggestion is during setup, create a user with ADMIN only rights. Do not assign it Super Admin rights. Reserve that for the super admin only. Store the super admin user id and password you created in a safe place and never give it out. Only use it if necessary, logging in using your user admin for day to day operations.

Avoid Weak Passwords—they are easily compromised

Closing Words

As you approach the design or maintenance of your site, quality is not something you install; quality must be designed in.

In this chapter we learned about Dr. Deming, one of the fathers of modern quality processes who clearly underscore's the point that you must forever and constantly improve your security. Not simply install a patch and go, but rather create processes that support a quality effort.

Patching, removing at-risk code and scanning your log files are only part of the process for improvement. You should also build a strong outer defense using .htaccess. Using .htaccess protects your sites from the parts of the world you don't want getting in. Yet those you want in are prevented from harming you through the use of strong passwords and proper file and directory permissions, completing the security gambit.

By making quality part of your process, using uptime as your measurement, will help your site to remain intact and safe.

Topics covered in this chapter

- Ensure you have the minimum safe version of Joomla!™
- What .htaccess is and how to set up a wall of protection
- What permissions are and how to set them
- The 6 basic steps each site administrator should conduct
- Remove any AT-RISK components
- The fact that *this is a battle* and you must be prepared

Chapter 3

Backup and Restoration

Creating a fall back position

Why read this chapter

When ever backups are discussed they are spoken of as necessary evil in hushed tones. Something you must do but don't want anything to do with. Successful backups lead to successful restorations. All sites at sometime will experience a loss in data and will require for what ever reason restoration. This restoration of course comes as I said from a successful backup.

This entire chapter is focused on the subject of backup and restoration.

Learning goals in this chapter

- The discussion of elements that comprise a successful backup
- Backup scenarios such as FULL and INCREMENTAL
- Detailed instruction on two methods of doing a BACKUP
- Backing up of core files, database, templates, and more
- Taking your media offsite and documenting it
- Conducting a restoration of the site, its core files and the database

Backup and Restoration

After crossing rivers
You must distance
Yourself from them
Do not tarry

Sun Tzu—The Art of War
Maneuvering Armies

Understanding what Sun Tzu was speaking of in this quote is critical to your backup and restoration strategy. In battle when an army reaches a river, Sun Tzu strongly recommended crossing as soon as possible. The reasons are many, but two come to mind; the first being if half your troops are in the water and half out, the enemy could easily overwhelm either half using different methods causing you to lose the battle. Another is if the river is on the rise, you could be swept away mounting the possibility of devastating loss of life.

How this relates to your backup strategy is that the troops crossing the river represent your backup media. Do not tarry after you cross the river has the meaning for us that you should remove your backup media as soon as possible from your backup site.

You can imagine the various reasons why you want to remove backup media. Yet just removing it is not enough. It needs to be labeled, documented as to what is on it, where it is going and who has it, your documents should clearly state, how to get it back for restoration purposes. If you can't retrieve it, you can't restore it.

The concept of a ***fall back position*** is the idea that during a battle, you may be forced back by the enemy. Your fall back position is where you are strongest and safest. The place the enemy is least likely to follow you. Backups *are your fall back position*

Remember a successful restoration is only as good as a successful backup. This chapter will focus on the different types of backups, *full,* and *incremental.* You will learn two methods to conduct a backup of your data and your database. Joomla!™ is comprised of two portions that need to be backed up. Joomla!™ the actual files, code, scripts and so on that you FTP up to your server. The second part is the actual database that keeps the content that is rendered on the screen. It is important that you capture both for a *full backup.*

Should a restoration become necessary you will decide on using the partial or full method to restore. We deal with the full method of restoration in this book due to the concept that if you are restoring, you have either failed for some reason or been attacked. I feel that if you have a good full backup, employ it even though it may take more time. The results will be a better outcome of your site.

Admin focus: Backups gone bad

Any backup strategy that is local and is working very well should have an archive process. That said choosing your remote site for archiving is as important as the backup. This story of a devastating fire in the London and Canadian storage facilities for data archive company Iron Mountain®, only highlights that you cannot solely depend on a copy of an off site backup. *Note the following headlines:*

"Iron Mountain fires prompt users to hasten hunt for backup options"[1]

"Iron Mountain London facility fire expected to result in full loss of records contained within the record centre"[2]

I cite this tragic occurrence with a footnote. The Iron Mountain facility® in Canada burned within a day or two of the London facility and the cause as of this time of writing according to news reports is unknown but appears coincidental. You need to consider contingencies in your disaster preparedness plan. Even to the degree of losing your backup media storage site.

Another backup gone bad story is one I am familiar with personally. While working at a large defense contractor in the late nineteen-eighties in computer systems maintenance, I received a panicked call from a customer about the loss of their disk drive. Upon arriving I found out that they had regularly backed up the project data nightly. I went through their procedures and did not note any problems with how they were conducting backups. The issue was they had lost a hard drive, a whopping *5 1/4"* 72 Megabyte hard drive and they were attempting to restore the data. The tape they were restoring from was good, as well as the tape device and software. The machine was healthy, yet the data would not come back.

It seems that the person conducting the local backups did what was known at that time as an *image backup*. This is where you copy the entire image of the hard drive with the intention of restoring it exactly as it had come off the drive. It turns out that *image backups* rarely, if ever, worked. It is moot to discuss why a vendor would knowingly ship a broken product, just accept that it sometimes happens.

Test early, test often, test and document and test again.

The real moral of the story here is the backups were conducted nightly and the tape stored safely away. They never *tested* the restore of the tape and had no process or plan to do so. Had they tested it they would have found out immediately that it would not work and chosen a *full* or *incremental* backup strategy instead; choosing to do a fresh restore of the operating system and applications, then restoring data.

---

[1]   http://www.computerworld.com/action/article.do?command=viewArticleBasic&articleId=9002051 (accessed July 2006)

[2]   http://www.continuitycentral.com/news02686.htm (accessed July 2006)

Backup scenarios

Full Backups

A full backup is a copy of all the files on the server (*your portion of the server*) every backup cycle. This however may not be necessary if your data is not changing often. In the case of Joomla!™ if you are not changing the actual underlying componetry, modules and plug-in's then an incremental backup copy of your DB should be fine for regular backups. You have to make the determination of the rate of data change for your scenario.

Consider also the number of sites you may have to do backup's for. The time to do one backup is multiplied by the number of sites you have.

Incremental Backups

The changes that occur on a daily basis are known as the *delta*, incremental backups only copy (usually) the deltas since the last full backup. Given the nature of Joomla!™ the fact that content is stored in a database lends itself to a Monday through Friday 'incremental' backup of the DB and a full backup on a weekend of all files and database content.

Usage of TAPE as a backup medium

If you use actual tape media, you will want to consider a rotation schedule for your tapes. Typically you would reuse an incremental tape every four or five weeks, while FULL backup's for archived storage are rarely reused. This will vary with your data protection (i.e. backup) policy. Keeping in mind though that tape has a fairly high degree of failure. In fact approximately five to twenty percent of backup and restoration jobs fail on a regular basis.[3]

Irreplaceable data from your site

Part of your backup strategy rests on knowing what data can be backed up (*optional*) and what data must be backed up (*vital to your site and cannot be replaced easily*).
For instance, do you have more than one site to manage? Is the data unique? Most likely it is and they will require their own backup.

More than one database?

Don't forget other tables in your database or even a second, third, etc, database on the same site.

---

[3] http://www.emc.com/products/systems/clariion_disk/pdf/meta_p2190.pdf (accessed September 2006)

Backing up core files and data on your Joomla!™ Site

If you performed a backup of the database, you would have what is termed an incremental backup of the site. Likewise if you backed up just the core files or the data but not the database you would have an incremental backup as well.

To conduct a full backup you would need to make a copy of all the files housed on your site as well as the contents of the database itself. Done correctly a full backup is easy and has a high degree of success and reliability.

EXAMPLE:

1. Create a folder or subdirectory on your LOCAL workstation.
    *   Label it backups
    *   Under the backups directory create a weekly folder such as:
        Wkly Aug 01, 2006

Using this method will assist you in restoring your site to a point before the loss or attack.

2. using your FTP program connect to your site with administrative privileges.

3. Highlight all the files and directories—making sure you get them all.

4. Download or *copy* all the files to your workstation to the backup location.

5. The next step is to pull that backup to a CD, DVD or tape and label it according to your standards and store it off site. Use the *Backup media offsite storage form, document number OSS-1000-A* to document your backups enabling you to retrieve them.

Example of a LABEL for your backup media.

> ***Backup set: August 1, 2007***
> ***FULL Backup***
> ***Site name: www.yourdomain.com***

This book is focused on Joomla!™-based sites running on a Linux O/S. While Joomla!™ will run on Windows® based servers, the procedures for backing up may be different. There are many tools available for Windows® platforms that allow real time and near real time copying of data to another location.

If you are running your site on a Windows® server platform you may consider investigating NSI Doubletake® (**see http://www.nsisoftware.com**). While this tool is not for everyone or every application it does have a great deal of features that may be useful to you for your platform.

Backup Methods for your Joomla!™ database

In this book we discuss two methods to conduct backups.

Method-1 Use PhpMyadmin to conduct your backups—if you are not comfortable using PhpMyadmin **please use** *method two*.

Method-2 Using the 3rd party extension **ebackup** available at *www.joomla.org*.

Each of these methods will conduct and provide an identical backup of your database. This *file* represents the sum total of your database from your site. This is fifty percent of your restoration needs, yet it is the most important. Keeping that file safe, up to date and easily retrieved is the goal of these two methods.

The first method is a very manual method and could be used for one off type of backups.

The second method is a third party extension and offers several advantages such as timed backups, capability to e-mail the DB backup file to you as well as a easy to use interface.

While both of these scenarios will work just fine to backup your database, you ultimately must decide which of the two work the best for you.

Method one—Using phpMyAdmin

Backup method One

Using the PHPMYADMIN tool to conduct a backup of the DB.

In this method you must have access to your PHPMYADMIN console to make a dump of your database.

Step 1 Making a backup of your database.

1. Login to your hosts control panel and open phpMyAdmin™

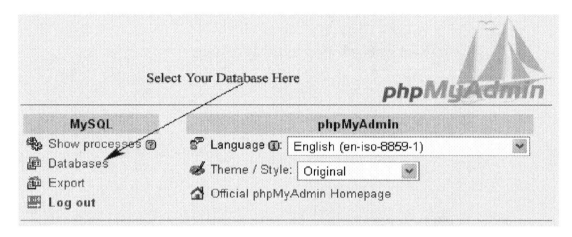

2. Select the database name you wish to backup. In our example it is Yc101DB

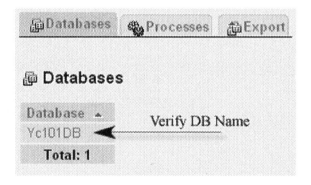

Method 1 Backup continued

3. Click on EXPORT

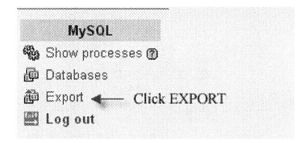

4. Select the Check all to highlight all the tables in your database

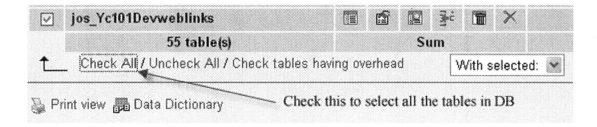

5. After which you will see this screen. Click on EXPORT again

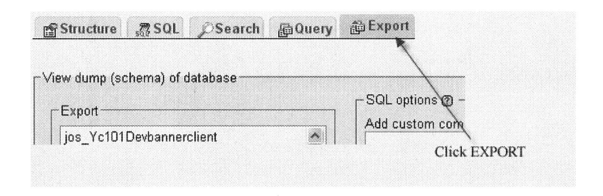

Method 1 Backup continued:

6. Make sure these boxes are checked.

Check these boxes:

Export
—Choose SQL as your dump format

Structure
—Add AUTO_INCREMENT value
—Enclose table and field names with back quotes

Data
—Use Hexadecimal for binary fields

Method 1 Backup continued:

7. Check the SAVE AS FILE BOX Make sure you select the "gzipped" button

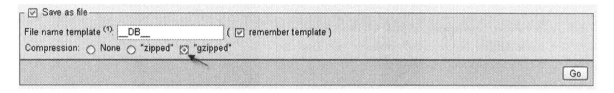

8. Your browser should open a save file dialog box. Enter where you would like this file saved.

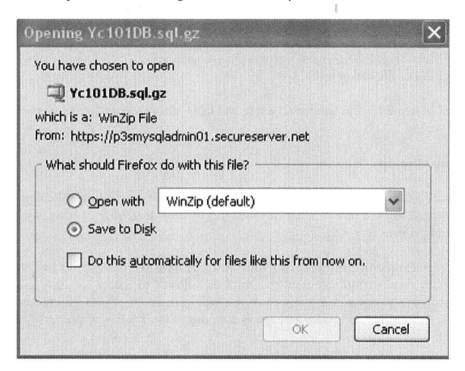

Method 1—Steps recapped

1. Login to host control panel—open phpMyAdmin
2. Select database you wish to backup
3. Click EXPORT
4. On the second screen that appears, click EXPORT again
5. Click the **Check All** field to select all tables in the database
6. Ensure you have selected all these boxes:

> *EXPORT*—Choose SQL as your dump format
> *STRUCTURE*—Add AUTO_INCREMENT VALUE
> —Enclose table and field names with back quotes
> *DATA*—Use hexadecimal for binary fields.

7. Check the SAVE AS FILE BOX—make sure you choose "gzipped"
8. Save file using browser file dialog box

The file you saved in step 8 IS your database, be sure and label, document and store off site.

Method 1 Backup wrap up

This method can be used as often as you like. This is great if you only have a single site that is very static and does not change often. You can just do a backup with this method as needed. Barring any unforeseen issues this method should perform very well.

The downside is that if you only use it once in a while you may have to break out this book to remember how to do it. Additionally there are multiple steps that must be followed to ensure you have a successful backup. Complementing this knowledge within these pages you will learn about proper maintenance and upkeep of your website. The need to patch, update and test is a method that if followed precisely, can prevent problems.

Method two—Using the 3rd party Extension—ebackup

Method Two—Using the 3rd party tool—eBackup

The next method discussed is using an extension known as ***eBackup***[4]. Personally I like this tool as it automates the backup process and gives you a consistent output.

As I write this I had a backup DB show up in my e-mail sent by this tool to me. This enables me to pull the backup out of e-mail, store on a thumb drive, cd, DVD or tape and lock away in my fireproof safe.

eBackup allows the administrator to schedule backups and have them archived on your site and e-mailed to you for offsite safe keeping. The component can be obtained from the joomla.org site.

Step 1—Install the component onto your site.

NOTE: this tool as of time of writing is currently listed as BETA, while we have tested it extensively, we are not and cannot guarantee it's performance or failure on your site.

Step 2—Open the COMPONENTS-EBACKUP—BACKUP on your site.
Step 3—Click the TABLES check box to select all the tables:

Step 4—Click the CHECK button—everything should be ok, if not it will be noted.

Step 5—RUN BACKUP JOB—REPEAT STEP 4 then press:

---

    4   ebackup copyright © 2006 by Mambobaer.de

Method 2 backup procedure—concluded

Settings	
Table Structure	☑
With 'DROP TABLE'	☑
With 'IF NOT EXISTS'	☑
Add AUTO_INCREMENT-Value	☑
Complete 'INSERT's	☑
Compress as gzip	☑
MySQL Export-Compatibility	MYSQL40 ▾
Comments/Settings Dialog	☑
Only environment tables (jos_jabber100)	☑
Max. Script Runtime (sec)	15
Delay for next session (ms)	5
eMail Address for transfer	book@joomlaspyder.com

Once you complete this step your backup will be e-mailed to you and stored online in the repository. It is important to check all the boxes you see in the above example.

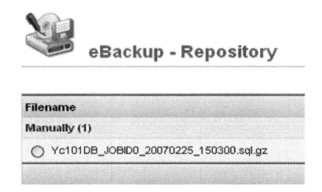

Filename
Manually (1)
○ Yc101DB_JOBID0_20070225_150300.sql.gz

Our latest (*and all*) backups can be found in the repository—note.
This IS stored on your site and should be backed up for safe keeping.

Our next step is to do a complete backup of the actual files, templates and data.

Moving the backup media off site—Instructions

Now that you have conducted a successful backup, you need to move the media offsite to a safe location where it can be protected from harm. The *backup media* offsite storage form is used to document your media, ensuring an accurate retrieval of media for restoration.

Fields on the backup media off site form.

- **Site URL:** This is the site URL you are backing up.
- **Name of company or location:** Company or location
- **Address fields:** Address where it is located, suite, unit and locker are for your discretion
- **Facility Access Information:** If this is a rented facility, such as a storage unit, what hours are they open? Additionally, what times can the media be retrieved.
- **Contact information:** These fields are to list the contact name(s), phone numbers, and account information such as account number, passwords or other security codes.
- **Authorized users:** Who has the authorization to retrieve the media and their contact information.
- **What type of media will you be storing:** Document the media type, such as tape or hard drive media. Under this field list the types of special handling, such as climate controlled or packed in foam for shock absorbency for instance.
- **What are the labeling standards for this backup?** It is important to define a label standard and use it consistently. Document it here.

Use of these fields is of course dependent on your particular situation and not all of them may apply.

<u>Backup media offsite storage</u>   Site URL: _____

Part One: Address, contact, Hours

Address where the backup media is stored:

_____

_____

Name of company: _____   Telephone: _____ X_____

Contact 1: _____   Contact 2: _____

Location attributes: (y/n)

Water proof? ____   Fire proof/protected? ____   Static guarded: ____   Secure? __ Open 24/7 ____

If facility is not open 24/7, what days/times is it open? Days_____ Times _____

Security information to drop off or pick up backup media.

Account/Auth num/._____   Passcode/Security Code _____

Authorized users	**Telephone #**	**Interaction allowed (y/n)**	**DR start up allowed (y/n)**
_____	_____	____	____
_____	_____	____	____
_____	_____	____	____

Part Two: What type of media will you be storing

Tape: **Hard media** ____   **Other media** _____

Dat: ____   **CD**   ____   **USB drive/Media: Size:** _____
DLT ____   **DVD**   ____   **Secured (y/n)**   _____
DDS ____   **Removable** ____   **Passcode:**   _____
Other _____ **Type:** _____

List special handling needs for media/Labeling standards for media

Restoration of a site due to compromise or other events

DO NOT ATTEMPT **method 2 if you are uncertain in any way about the quality of your data, documentation and skills. Contact your host and ask them to restore your site.**

The most critical task during a crisis is to _protect_ the data and then get your site back online.

The crisis and loss of data could be due to natural disaster, fire, flood, attack, malicious employees, hard drive failures or other items too numerous to mention.

There are an endless amount of scenarios resulting in data loss such the accidental deletion of a critical file; that is a simple restoration of that file. Take another scenario where you are cracked or attacked are you certain that simply removing the affected files and replacing them will fix it? Can you be sure that there isn't evil lurking somewhere? **The correct answer is if you cannot easily, then do a full restore.**

When that day comes you will need to be ready to initiate your plan as soon as possible to restore operations in the event of data loss.

In this section you will learn how to conduct a restore using the manual step by step method to resume operations on your site.

This method may not work if you have not properly, documented your working configuration, made regular backups of the database, or backed up specific data such as a highly modified template.

Again a successful restoration is only as good as the process of a successful backup.

The two methods described have forms to document the restoration of your data, later in this book.

Method 1: Your web host conducts the restoration.

Method 2: The manual method requiring your configuration, base code versions, SQL DB dump and 3rd party extensions be available for restore. This is done locally.

Admin Focus: 3rd Party restoration versus self-administered restoration

This topic is worthy of stopping to review in detail for the pro's and con's of each point.

Pro's of 3rd Party restoration	Con's of 3rd Party restoration
Someone else has the day to day responsibility of backing up and storing the tape or other media. This includes the real estate costs, labor costs and media costs, uptime, etc.	They may not have proper facilities or processes in place. The quality of their backup's, unless tested, is unknown.
Ability to make a phone call and start restoration processes	Their time frame may not match yours. It could be a "we'll restore tomorrow" type of service. There are probably costs associated for restoration.
The media is probably near your server's location—easy to access, well engrained process to their hosting and customer service process.	The media is probably near your server's location—ask the provider where they store it and how. If it's on site and there's a fire, there goes the backups as well.
Pro's of self-administered backups	**Con's of self-administered backups**
You can initiate a backup anytime. Making sure you have the latest in versions and so forth before you come back online.	Your backup may have had a Trojan horse on it for sometime and restoration without a process to check for cleanliness.
You are the master of your data, ensuring even the most sensitive of data is under your control.	As the master of your data you have the responsibility to make sure backups are conducted regularly, moved offsite, secured and documented. This can raise your administrative overhead greatly.

As you can see there are a few good and bad reasons on both sides of the fence. You can weigh out the value of each as you go through this process and decide on the proper path to take.

Method 1 Restoration

3rd party host to restoration
Of your site

Guideline for completing emergency restoration procedures form—3rd party hosted

On the following page you will collect all the information from your host that should be needed to request a restoration. Some hosts may have other requirements and if so use the second page of this form to record host specific information.

This page is a *scratch* or working form. You will use it to gather the information and transfer it to a duplicate form storing it in your DP book.

- **Site URL:** This is the specific site you are building this disaster preparedness around
- **Support Phone number:** This is a generic field that can be used for host, your internal tech support or a third party.
- **Option to reach support:** This is to document the IVR prompts of your support or HOST organization.
- **What are the costs to restore?** If your host charges a fee for restoration (many do) note the costs here.
- **What is the restoration time?** There is a lag between the time a job can be started and the restoration is finished. Contact your host to gather this information.
- **How often do they backup?** Contact the support group and ask them how often they backup.
- **Hosts procedure for backing up:** Contact your host and ask them what their procedures are. Additionally find out if they are tape, cd or low cost hard drive storage. Ask if they remove the backup media from their site to a safe location.
- **Account number:** List your specific account number
- **Passcode:** List your pin or password you will need to commence recovery
- **Other security information required (Two fields):** These are optional for your specific situation.
- **Approvals:** List first and second contacts in your organization who have the authority to call a disaster event and start the recovery.
- **Other important information for restoration:** This is a general section for things such as: "the keys for the server room are located with or at …", or "Contact building security immediately upon disaster commencement." The specifics of this portion will apply to you.

Emergency Restoration Procedures—Hosted pg 1 of 2   URL:

Support phone number: (   )   -   **Extension or option number:** _____

Restoration costs ($$$): _____   what is the restoration time?   _____ (hrs/mins)

HOSTING ONLY: How often does your host backup?
Nightly ____ Weekly _____ Monthly _____ Never _____

Hosts current procedure for backing up:

Security information I will need to give host to initiate restoration

Account number: _____   Password or Passcode: _____

Other: _____   Other: _____

Who can initiate the restoration?

First approval contact name: _____ Num: (   ) ____-_____

Second approval contact name: _____ Num: (   ) ____-_____

Other important information for restoration

Signature of primary approver   _____

Name of primary approver   _____

Signature of secondary approver _____

Name of secondary approver   _____

Emergency Restoration Procedures—Hosted pg 2 of 2   Site URL: _____

Confirmation that site is backup and functional _____

REQUIRED: Check site for malicious scripts, wrong revision code and other items that may cause site to incur further downtime or issues   Answer (y/n) ____

Scripts _____   **Down Revision** _____

Correct template _____   **Custom code back in place** _____

Signature of primary approver   _____

Name of primary approver   _____

Signature of secondary approver   _____

Name of secondary approver   _____

Method 2—Manual Restoration of your site

Method 2—Manual restoration from your own media

This method is considered for advanced users, and should only be used if you have documented your site properly, and have conducted successful backups, meaning you have tested for successful restorations, otherwise **do not attempt.**

Should your site experience an attack or you suspect it, you will need to fall back to your last known good backup media. As an example this means that if you were cracked on a Friday and you backed up weekly, you would want to go back to the Friday before the outage to commence restoration.

Step 1—Stop and determine the true nature of the situation

Determine first if you are truly cracked or down before you officially decide to restore. After you are certain you need to make sure you have gathered your backup media, DP book and your team members.

Using the following example as a test to see if your site is unreachable. Open your browser and visit www. megaproxy.com. Type in your site URL and see if your site is up, if so then the next step is to *ping* the server.

Example: Open a Command Prompt and
Type in PING <your sites IP address>
Or
PING <www.yourdomain.com>

You should see a similar output as this if everything is working.

Pinging yourdomain.com [192.168.1.010] with 32 bytes of data:

Reply from 192.168.1.010: bytes=32 time=47ms TTL=47
Reply from 192.168.1.010: bytes=32 time=53ms TTL=47
Reply from 192.168.1.010: bytes=32 time=46ms TTL=47
Reply from 192.168.1.010 bytes=32 time=47ms TTL=47

Ping statistics for 192.168.1.010

Packets: Sent = 4, Received = 4, Lost = 0 (0% loss),
Approximate round trip times in milliseconds:
Minimum = 46ms, Maximum = 53ms, Average = 48ms

Note to reader: Your address will be different

Method 2—Manual restoration from your own media—continued

Assuming you received valid return pings from your server then your next step should be to verify with your host there are not any other issues.

However assuming it was an attack or defacement then you will need to wipe out all files and do a restore from a clean backup. This means deleting everything on the site.

If you have been exploited, then your backups may have an exploit on them as well. Try to determine "when" you were attacked and select a backup before that time.

Here are the basic steps for recovery.

*   FTP into your site and wipe all directories and files from your site.
*   Restore the last Joomla!™ version you were using (if you were 1.0.12 then install 1.0.12).
*   Delete the database and recreate a new one or drop all the tables.
*   Reinstall all the components, modules, plugins, templates, mambots from your documented list of inventory.
*   Open phpMyAdmin and do a database restore.
*   Visit Joomla.org and download the latest Joomla!™ updates and install.
*   Test to ensure everything is ok.
*   Backup and follow offsite storage procedures.

What you have in effect done is wipe out any potentially hazardous scripts or code that may be waiting, replaced the Joomla!™ with fresh, clean Joomla!™, reinstalled all components and restored the database. This should restore all your content and settings.

If you have been keeping up with patches you may not have to follow this step but it is may be a good idea to do so.

Check versions of each installed 3rd party extension against the list on Joomla!™ located at:

http://forum.joomla.org/index.php/topic,79477.0.html

*   If any of your components are out of date, uninstall and delete them.
*   Reinstall the new components.

The following pages contain the pictorial guide and a check list form to step you through each action. The graphics on the following pages are examples; please follow the form to do a restoration.

Graphical guide for restoration of database

Open your phpMyAdmin from your control panel and select the SQL button.
Ensure that it says: **No tables found in database**

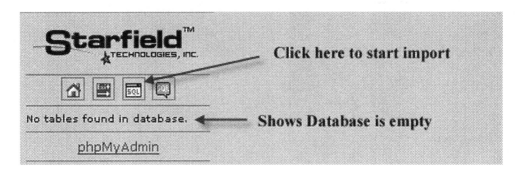

Next select the Import Files tab as seen below, select BROWSE to find your file

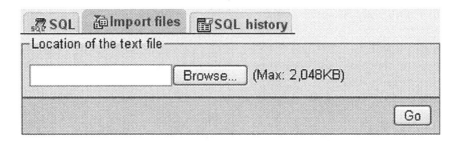

Select the .SQL file of your chosen backup

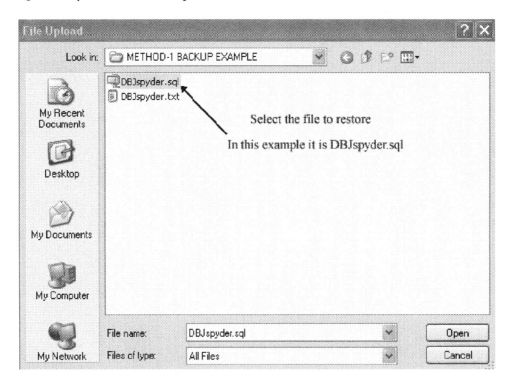

Graphical guide for restoration of database

Once the tables have been imported you will see a message that indicates success.

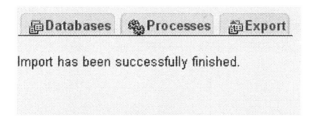

At this point you are ready to do the actual restoration of the database tables. Follow the check list on the next page to do so.

The signature forms at the top are clearly your choice, however they are highly recommended. As part of your disaster plan you need to have a person who is accountable with a backup (preferably two iterations of backups) who can initiate this type of a recovery.

Caution: AS STATED EARLIER IF YOU ARE NOT COMFORTABLE AND CONFIDENT IN YOUR BACKUPS, SKILL LEVEL OR ANY OTHER ISSUE THAT MAY PREVENT A SUCCESSFUL RESTORATION DO NOT ATTEMPT THIS. CONTACT YOUR HOST PROVIDER TO DO A RESTORATION OF YOUR SITE.

Restoration steps—recap

- FTP into your site and wipe all directories and files from your site.
- Restore the last Joomla!™ version you were using (if you were 1.0.12 then install 1.0.12).
- Delete the database and recreate a new one or drop all the tables.
- Reinstall all the components, modules, plugins, templates, mambots from your documented list of inventory.
- Open phpMyAdmin and do a database restore.
- Visit Joomla.org and download the latest Joomla!™ updates and install.
- Test to ensure everything is ok.
- Backup and follow offsite storage procedures.

Restoration checklist & signoff form   Date of event: _____   Time: _____

Signature of primary approver _____
Name of primary approver   _____

Signature of secondary approver _____
Name of secondary approver   _____

Step	Action required	Completed

1.   Media retrieved and label verified
2.   FTP into server, wipe directory
3.   Download minimum safe Joomla!™
4.   Refer to your site inventory forms
5.   Download the LATEST SAFE level of the components on step four
6.   Delete the old database
7.   Recreate the database and record the database settings on the next line

DB Name: _____   DB Passcode:_____

Host Name: _____   Other DB info: _____

Creation of database verified (y/n) ____

8.   Install the minimum safe Joomla!™ base code
9.   Install the minimum safe Components, Modules, Plugin/mambots and templates
10.   Install any mandatory specialized code
11.   Login into your host control panel and start phpMyAdmin.
12.   You should see: **No tables found in database.**
13.   Click the SQL button
14.   Click the Import Files Button
15.   Dialog box will ask you for the location of the TEXT file—browse and select
16.   After Selection press GO and tables will be imported
17.   Open your **configuration.php** file and make sure DB name matches step 7 above
18.   After you have completed these steps refer to the test matrix to run a complete SITE wide test.

Signature of primary—Actions above are complete   _____

Name of primary approver   _____

Signature of secondary—Actions above are complete   _____

Name of secondary approver   _____

Backup policies

If you are managing sites other than your own then work with your customer to develop a policy statement. This will help to keep you out of hot water if a file is not backed up yet someone feels as it should have been.

These items are a subset of larger customer policy that is beyond the scope of this book. These should get you started on the road to discussing the backups with your customers. Consider these items as you create your own policy.

- What websites will be backed up? Treat each site to be backed up as separate and unique.
- Ensure with your customer or client that the policy covers the specific data that is required to be backed up and restored. For instance if they do not care about the base load of Joomla!™ document this fact and make sure it is signed off by the customer.
- Determine the frequency of incremental and full backups. The more media you backup the more costs to store it, and the likely hood of getting the wrong media during a crisis unless you have a good process to label, document, store and retrieve the media. This is why the concept of a labeling standard is part of this plan. Make sure to follow it.
- Who has sign off authority to initiate a full restore? If it is you, as determined by your customer, make sure this is documented and signed off.
- When will you rotate backup media into use? Some data backups will be so obsolete over a period of time it only makes sense to destroy the backup media as in the case of highly sensitive data or to recycle, label the media and put it into use again. Work with your customer to determine how long they wish to keep backup media. If you are the customer then make the determination based on how frequently the data changes and how long you feel you need backup copies.

These only represent a few things to think through as you establish a written backup policy. A good backup policy will keep you out of political hot-water when push comes to shove; **make sure you create one**.

Closing Words

As I penned these closing words I read over the articles about the terrible fires in the Iron Mountain® facilities. This type of occurrence should give every reader pause to consider 'what if?' What if your procedures for backup were faulty? What would happen if you lost your server and did not even have a backup? What if the location you have your backup media in burned down?

In this chapter we learned about different types of backups as well as different methods of restorations of lost data. My chef-wife told me a story about recipes that I think applies here. In a nutshell, in order to replicate a good recipe over and over, providing the diner with a consistently attractive and delicious meal, you have to document the ingredients, the preparation steps, cooking and serving methods, then follow it.
The same thing actually applies to backups.

The point is the entire purpose of the backup is to be restored at some later date. To do this involves choosing a means to restore, labeling the backup media consistently and storing it offsite (away from your server). Document your process, test and retest. This will give you a solid recovery model for your data.

Topics covered in this chapter

- How to backup your database
- How to backup your core files
- How to document for removal and off site storage your media
- In the event of disaster conducting a successful restoration

Chapter 4

Site Readiness

Maintenance of your Joomla!™ site

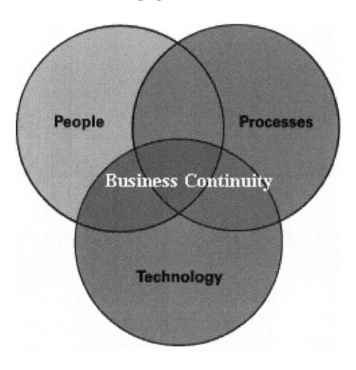

Why read this chapter

This chapter covers the concepts of maintaining your site. This means keeping up with patches, good security practices and 3rd party code.

Learning goals in this chapter

In most well run IT shops there is a set of written policies covering the standards of operations.

It defines at a minimum:

- Who does what
- When they do it
- How they do it
- On occasion why they do it.

In this chapter you will learn methods on the when, who and why.

Included in this chapter are forms to help you conduct maintenance.

Readying the Troops

You must learn through planning.
You must question the situation.
You must ask.
Which government has the right philosophy?
Which commander has the right skill?
Which season and place has the right advantage?
Which method of command works?
Which group of forces has the strength?
Which officers and men have the training?
Which rewards and punishments make sense?
This tells when you will win and when you will lose.
Some commanders perform this analysis.
If you use these commanders, you will win.
Keep them.
Some commanders ignore this analysis.
If you use these commanders, you will lose.
Get rid of them.

Sun Tzu on leadership and planning

Planning and executing maintenance is no different than the above passage from Sun Tzu. I have spent over twenty years in the computer business at the vendor level working on such pieces of equipment as, mainframes, mini's, wide-area and local area networks, microwave uplinks/downlinks, PC's, servers, various operating systems and storage area networks. My career started out of college doing component level repair of barcode readers. A very short time later I moved into a computer system maintenance position with a defense contractor and from there into presales technical support for two major computer vendors. Having seen the effects of good and bad maintenance practices I want you to draw from my experiences to help you craft a strong maintenance strategy.

Why maintenance? Any OS, software, bios, code, script, and applications tend to *rot*. In other words, they tend to age ungracefully, often quickly. As soon as an exploit is discovered it makes it way around the world in hours. Often times using these exploits against average people who are faceless, nameless *targets* to the enemies of our websites. Your site is no different in its needs to be maintained than any system.

Proper maintenance is important to perform and conduct according to a regular schedule. If your site were a car, would you drive it to the oil-change shop after the oil light came on? Some people might, however I doubt they will pay attention to this book.

In this chapter you will be introduced to an easy-to-follow schedule to keep your site maintained, healthy, and prepared in the event of a disaster.

Opening

What is the definition of maintenance?[1]

Dictionary.com defines it in this way:

> **The act of maintaining or the state of being maintained.**
> **The work of keeping something in proper condition; upkeep.**
>
> **It further defines the word in terms of software as:**
>
> **<Programming> The modification of a software product, after**
> **delivery, to correct faults, to improve performance or other**
> **attributes, or to adapt the product to a changed environment.**

If you reread the quote from Sun Tzu, you could liken his instruction to good or bad maintenance procedures. If your procedures are good, they are like the good commander. You should keep them. If your maintenance practices and procedures are bad or even non-existent then they are like the bad commander. You should rid yourself of them.

Ignoring maintenance of your site is only going to get you in trouble. The focus of this chapter is to learn what good maintenance is. Forget what bad maintenance is because it will go by the wayside when you implement good procedures.

Want more reasons to conduct regular maintenance?

From July 2003 through June 2005, the average number of published computer vulnerabilities was around 2500 per year or nearly six to seven each day. Even if you only have a single server you should expect to spend time reviewing a handful of critical patches per month.

Putting in a maintenance process

You will find within this chapter several forms that help you with daily, weekly and monthly tasks including backing up database and site code.

Once you examine these forms you may use the ones in the back of the book or download a set from our site at *www.joomspyder.com.*

---

[1]   maintenance. Dictionary.com. *Dictionary.com Unabridged (v 1.1)*. Random House, Inc. http://dictionary.reference.com/browse/maintenance (accessed: December 01, 2006)

Maintenance works for everything.

During the writing of this chapter I recalled the time when I was going to college, I worked as a maintenance man at a chain of nursing home facilities. I worked with a senior employee, Edgar, who had many years experience in maintaining air conditioners, heaters, electrical, plumbing, and more. In fact I never saw anything that Edgar could not fix or repair.

What an opportunity for me to learn skills that would become a staple of my knowledgebase. The interesting thing is I did not realize those skills I was acquiring would play a large role in my IT career.

You see each room had an individual air conditioner mounted in the wall. The kind you might see at a nice hotel. One hot afternoon, Edgar told me we were going to *wash the air conditioners*. I chuckled, and went with him thinking that was a joke; it clearly was not. We unplugged each unit, opened it, and using a water hose we cleaned the metal grills in the unit. Edgar explained to me that dirt, dust and debris fills up the grill keeping the air from flowing *into* the unit. Making the ac compressor work that much harder, and shortening its life, consuming more electricity, and delivering less cool air to the room.

There were many other examples such as that, but they all revolved around the theme of maintaining the building, equipment, vehicles, washers, dryers, stoves, or whatever the equipment was to keep it at its peak operating efficiency. Most people understand that because they can see it, and touch it. It is a tangible thing that they know exists.

Software is no different except you cannot really see it. A lot of people don't think about maintenance until a crisis happens or it breaks down. Then the difficult task of returning the systems or sites back to working order, causing frustration on the part of employees, customers, and you.

As you move through this chapter keep in mind the lesson learned from washing the air conditioning units was not fun, but clearly extends the life of the units, and helped to keep the residents cool.

Your site properly maintained will much more than likely be error, and problem free and keep the customers and visitors cool.

Maintenance

Why—

In the opening of this chapter it was stated that you wouldn't drive your car to the oil change shop only after the oil light came on. If you did, the chances of your engine being severely damaged would be very high. The engine requires regular maintenance of fluids, belts, moving parts, and so on helping to keep it running at optimum levels.

Joomla!™ is the engine of your site. Let's say that as you read this you are still running older code, chances are great that your site could be exploited or attacked by predator technical terrorists, and criminals on the Internet using well-documented, well-known methods.

Some exploits, which go unnoticed, are meant to turn your site into a SPAM relay or *spam-bot*. They may be after personal information or they may run *kiddie-scripts* just to see if they can break into your site for fun.

How—

This is the part that gets most administrators bogged down. Security is all too often an afterthought when setting up, and running sites and servers and conducting business. Mismanagement or "non-maintenance' of one small component can have disastrous effects

When—

As often as needed-that's when. When phrased like that most administrators, know that is correct, but glaze over. "I don't have time." "It won't happen to me." "We have firewalls".

> *Wake up—this is the Internet. It's a living, changing entity day in-day out.*

Where—

Joomla!™ core: Keep up to date with patches and security releases—
3rd party extensions: Read up on www.joomla.org to review the latest information

> *"Just because you're not paranoid, doesn't mean they aren't after you."—Anonymous.*

Daily—Weekly—Monthly maintenance

Weekly

- Keep an eye on the server logs (if you have access to them). Watch for anything 'out of the ordinary'— While that's a general statement watching them daily will give you an idea of what to expect; allowing you to respond to things that are not ordinary.
- Login once a day just to ensure no defacement happened, and ensure the site is up.
- Document the changes to any configuration files, ini files, template, etc.
- Perform a *full* or *incremental* file backup of the site files.
- Perform a *full database* backup.
- Take (if possible) a copy of the backup files offsite
- If your host backs up, ask for a copy of their backup/restoration schedule/plan.
- Read the Joomla!™ Security forum to see if any hot topics have come up.

Monthly

- Review the security forums for exploits.
- Review the components/mods/plugins related to YOUR site.
- Change all administrative passwords, including the database, ftp, the core admin and any others such as RSS feeds.
- Optional but highly recommended: Change your users passwords.

Other

- This form is for needs specific to your site only.

Maintenance Forms—Overview

The maintenance charts have been developed with the thought in mind of helping the administrator track upkeep of their sites. These forms are designed to help you by documenting the tasks of the site needs. They define tasks needed to keep your site in great working order, and give you a structured means to collect the information.

The intended use of these forms is based in the concept of creating a process that works, by following it every time in order to deliver a quality product. In the manufacturing of a product often times quality is believed to be "inspected in" yet quality is not something that you can inspect in. It is either there, or not at the time a product is built. There must be a process to design quality in at the start.

Don't forget to visit www.joomspyder.com to download a set of generic forms or purchase a set of custom forms and DP handbook.

Maintenance forms

Instructions for using the maintenance forms

The following is a description of each form and its purpose.

Weekly:
There are important things that you must do weekly, such as backing up, labeling your media, and removing it to an offsite location. Doing a full backup of all core files, data, and databases are a once a week task. The form will address each of these items.

Document number W-1000-M

Monthly:
Your site requires good security administration on a regular maintenance. The monthly form helps you with those security issues that often are forgotten or overlooked. Here you will review the security forums, look for new releases, patches, etc. If available apply, and document the changes. Changing your passwords is a monthly task that you will need to perform.

Document number—M-1000-M

Other:
Since every site is unique we have included a generic form for you to add items for you or your staff that do not fall into the first two forms.

Document numbers—Gen-1000-A

Testing matrix
As new code is added, it should be tested, documented, rolled into production and tested again. These two forms provide the framework for documentation of this process.

Document number—TM-1000-A, PM-1000-A

Off site storage form:
Removal of backup media, and storage to an offsite location will enable you to recover from most disasters. This form documents the passwords, location, media type, labeling standards and any special needs

Document number—OSS-1000-A

Weekly Tasks   **Site URL:**   **Week of:**

	Verified site is up	Database Backed up	Files backed up	Type of backup
Mon				
Tues				
Wed				
Thur				
Fri				
Sat				
Sun				

Reviewed security forum: ___ y/n Applied patches: ___ Extension patched: _____

Notes for week about site:

Signed: _____ Name: _____

Date: __/__/__

Monthly Tasks   **URL:**   **Month:**   **Year:**

Version changes

Name: _____   Old version _____   New Version _____

Reason for change: _____

Name: _____   Old version _____   New Version _____

Reason for change: _____

Name: _____   Old version _____   New Version _____

Reason for change: _____

Passwords:

New admin password: _____   New admin password: _____

Forced user password change: _____ y/n

Backups:

Full backup completed and moved offsite/safe storage: _____ y/n

Monthly tasks that must be completed:

•

•

•

Signed: _____

Name:_____

Date: __/__/__   **Document number M-1000-M**

General Maintenance Log URL:_____ Date: __/__/__

Tasks that are unique to your site that need to performed:

TASK	NEEDS TO BE COMPLETED BY:

1.

2.

3.

4.

5.

6.

7.

8.

Who is responsible for these tasks: _____

Completed by (name) _____ **Signature:** _____

Document number—Gen-1000-A

Admin Focus   the tale of two sites

This admin focus is the story of poor administrative practices resulting in problems.

Customer one

This was a simple upgrade to the latest stats package in use. Upon upgrading the admin noticed that in daily use, monitoring stats would cause the browser to dump and error out. It only did this with non-IE browsers. Since the exact cause of these issues was unknown, it was decided to continue monitoring. It turns out that due to the use of Flash to generate graphing, a bug in the non-IE browser caused it to shutdown. By turning off graphing it resolved the problem. Of course moving to Internet Explorer®, and leaving graphing on would accomplish the same thing. The issue it seems was with NON-IE browsers. Proper testing methodology would have caught this and prevented this issue.

Customer two

The second site is a very busy site, with a popular forms package on it. The owner of the site began putting out radio advertisement causing even heavier traffic. The form was used to register customers for a seminar, and the form had stopped working.

Recently the admin had installed a third party search engine friendly (SEF) component. During this "mini-disaster" the resolution was found by going to the form vendor's site, noting that the component had not been tested, and stated it may not work. After turning off the SEF component, the form extension began working immediately. The right thing to do would have been to research the forms vendors site to see if there were any known issues or if it was even tested, which it was clearly not.

The point of both these is the admin did not follow the rules. He like everyone else is human and mistakenly approached these situations without a plan.

When you are ready to upgrade or add extensions follow these steps

1. Load up your new component or upgrade on a 'sandbox' version of your site
2. Draw up a TEST matrix
3. Thoroughly test EACH function of the site using your test matrix.
4. If you note any anomalies, do not implement.
5. If you think it is all working do a search on the forums for the component vendor and Joomla!™ to see if there is anything you missed.
6. If you feel it is ready to go, follow the steps for your site, install and then retest against the test matrix.

Test sites VS production sites

Instructions for using Test Matrix Forms—Development environment

Two forms are provided for testing. One is for testing or development in your sandbox. This form is document number **TM-1000-A**

The second form is to retest your results in your production environment. This is important due to the fact that your production environment may not match your development or test environment exactly. This document is numbered **PM-1000-A**.

The *Development/Sandbox* form is intended for you to use in testing any upgrades, patches, etc before rolling to production. The top portion is for you to fill out the site name, the name of the upgraded software, and listing what type of extension it is.

The middle portion of the form is to list all the current installed pieces, and *their* version numbers. It is important that you go through and list each one because there might be an occasion where your production site did not match your sandbox site. This will enable you to track down any issues or mismatches quickly and easily.

The last section is for you to indicate any problems noted, such as "after installing/upgrading the module "Y", the component "X" no longer works." You can list corrective actions taken.

If you are satisfied with the test, move to the next form and roll it out to production.

Development site test form   URL: _____

Joomla!™ Version installed:

Name of upgraded software: **Version number:**

Production? _____ **y/n**

Check what it is: Component __   Module __   Plugin/Mambot __   Template __

List components, modules, plug-ins, mambots installed

Name: **Version**   **Name**   **Version:**

_____

_____

_____

_____

_____

Will this upgrade require end user training? _____ **y/n**

If **YES** has training been scheduled before rollout? ___ **y/n**

After upgrading are all portions of the site verified to be up and running? _____

List any areas that are not running properly:

Any problems noted/corrective actions taken.

Instructions for using Test Matrix Forms—Production environment

While this form is similar, and it seems that you are duplicating work the purpose is to make you go through the production site and list anything running. You might have a slight difference between your sandbox versus your live site and this will help you catch it.

After you install the new software, you will go through your site and test again to verify whether each part works or not. Again, while this may seem redundant, it is possible that your development environment does not match exactly your production environment.

Once all upgrades, testing and user acceptance are completed, you can note corrective actions that were taken if necessary and that this is stable for production release.

When you are administrating multiple sites or a single site the better your documentation of what has occurred in the past, the better the chances of recovery in a disaster.

These two forms, *Development* and *Production*, are important tools for administration of your sites.

User acceptance testing

One accepted method of qualification is a *user acceptance test, w*hich according to Dr. Rittenghouse's book, ***Managing Software Deliverables***[2] is defined as:

> ***"Formal testing conducted to determine whether or not a system satisfies its acceptance criteria and to enable the user to determine whether or not to accept the system."***

User acceptance testing should be an integral part of your success criteria. This could be used if you are a designer for other's sites as well. Giving you a bit of protection if they sign off and later it breaks. They won't be able to say that you did not test it as they verified it. This will give you a wonderful base to find errors, and the end users will find problems you may or may not see as well.

---

2   Rittenhouse, John W, PhD, CISM "Managing Software Deliverables-A software development management methodology" (Digital Press, Oxford, UK), 258

Production site verification form   **URL:**

Joomla!™ Version installed: _____   Name of upgraded software:
Version number: Put into production? _____ **y/n**

Check what it is: Component __   Module __   Plugin/Mambot __   Template __

List components, modules, plug-ins, mambots installed

Name: Version   Name   Version:

_____

_____

_____

_____

_____

User acceptance testing/Sign off as good for production

Does this upgrade require user or customer acceptance? _____ **y/n**

Have any problems with the production environment been noted? ____ **y/n**

If so has corrective action been taken? _____ **y/n**

Is this stable for production release? ____ **y/n**

User: Signed _____ Name _____ Date _____

Admin: Signed _____ Name _____ Date _____

Moving your backup media offsite

Part of a good preparedness plan is access to offsite storage of media. In corporate America there are many companies built around that very need. They retrieve, store and deliver backup and recovery media.

While you may not have the needs of such a service, you do have a responsibility to remove backup media offsite to a safe location.

The offsite media form is to help with the removal of media to a secured location giving you a single place to record all the particulars. This will become part of your disaster preparedness plan. Remember, this form is a *scratch* or practice form. All of the forms are in the back of the book, and are available for download at **www. joomspyder.com.**

This form documents the names, addresses, times, and telephone numbers of the locations of where your media is stored. Included is an account or authorization code as well as any password or security codes that may be needed to retrieve or drop off the media. Authorized users who can drop off, and pickup the media are noted in this form.

Additionally the form addresses the media itself, in terms of the type of media, any special handling/storage it may require, and the labeling standards.

While I don't address the idea of how you should label your media, I advocate you create a standard method, and stick with it.

Once you have that, list it under the heading **LABELING STANDARDS FOR MEDIA**.

Note to the reader. The form on the following page is here to reflect the need for maintenance of back-ups being moved offsite. It is repeated elsewhere in the book.

Backup media offsite storage   Site URL: _____

Part One: **Address, contact, Hours**

Address where the backup media is stored:

_____

_____

Name of company: _____   Telephone: _____ X_____

Contact 1: _____   Contact 2: _____

Location attributes: (y/n)

Water proof? ____   Fire proof/protected? ____   Static guarded: ____   Secure? __ Open 24/7 ___

If facility is not open 24/7, what days/times is it open? Days_____ Times _____

Security information to drop off or pick up backup media.

Account/Auth num/._____   Passcode/Security Code _____

Authorized users	Telephone #	Interaction allowed (y/n)	DR start up allowed (y/n)
_____	_____	____	____
_____	_____	____	____
_____	_____	____	____

Part Two: **What type of media will you be storing**

Tape:	Hard media ___	Other media _____
Dat: ____	CD ___	USB drive/Media: Size: _____
DLT ____	DVD ___	Secured (y/n) _____
DDS ____	Removable ___	Passcode: _____
Other _____ Type: _____		

List special handling needs for media/Labeling standards for media

Closing Words

I listen to a car show in my area on the weekends where callers discuss issues about their automobiles. While not often, I have heard a caller from time to time ask what to do if their **check oil** light comes on.

If you know much of anything about auto's then you know that by the time the **check oil** light comes on the chances are good your engine is damaged.

Regular maintenance of your car includes checking the level of oil often. One way to ensure you have enough oil is to check the level when you fill up with gasoline. The day's of full service attendants who would check 'all the fluids' are gone; it's now up to you.

Your site is like that, no one is going to check for you. This means that maintenance must be a way of life. The purpose of this chapter was to help you develop a framework, and a guide to keep your site up to speed, guide to help you to *check the oil* on your site if you will.

In this chapter you were introduced to why, when and how you should conduct maintenance. Using the forms will give you an easy to follow process that is as simple as checking off a task list.

I cannot encourage you enough to do the proper maintenance of your site and your autos!

Good driving!

Topics covered in this chapter

- Gained an understanding of "WHY"
- Gained an good understanding of "HOW"
- Gained an understanding of site maintenance.
- Put a solid framework together to maintain your site
- Regular maintenance can prevent most problems
- before they happen.

Chapter 5

Incident Reporting

How to ask for help and get it

Proper methods of reporting bugs and attacks to your site
To the Joomla!™ community and your ISP or host

Why read this chapter

Ask four people who are witness to an accident, the details and chances are you will get four distinct answers. It's the nature of being human, to process what you see within your unique frame of reference.

When you need to report an incident or seek help from the Joomla!™ forum, the amount of information you give is directly proportional to the amount of help you get.

When seeking help a structured method to gather, and react to the event is needed. This eliminates much of the subjective nature of reporting that often times in all technical fields results in bad customer experience metrics. This is not to say that tech support groups or forums are not on occasion at fault. It is to say that they cannot read your mind.

This chapter will give you a framework to gather the needed information to report events in a structured method; this will yield the fastest, and hopefully the best response.

Learning goals in this chapter

- **Proper methods of reporting problems to the Joomla!™ Community**
- **Proper methods of reporting problems to your HOST or your ISP**

"All that is needed for
The triumph of evil is that
Good persons
Do nothing."

Edmund Burke

*E*dmund Burke's words echo loud and clear in today's society. This chapter is devoted to the proper methods to collect information, report it to the Joomla!™ forum, your host or to ISP's when you are cracked. On the forums I have read opinions ranging from *it won't do any good* all the way to the *politically correct and dangerous accusation of racism* should you take an action towards stopping the malcontents. This simply is masking the problem under false pretense of *good-will* and should not be allowed. The perpetrators of crimes, no matter their country of origin, religion of choice or their skin color should have no bearing on enforcing the law and keeping them out of your site.

Many times an ISP is as innocent as you, and is being used as a relay to reach you only. That does not make you a racist to report a crack from a foreign telecom. It makes you a responsible netizen.

The fact often times is ISP's, and hosts find out where security holes are based on reports of attacks originating through, or from them.

If you are looking for help on the support forums, you can find many good people with answers to help you through any type of problem. This chapter will focus on helping you gather the details from your site, and about your problem for them to help you.

Use the forms in this chapter as a basis of reporting. The Joomla!™ Quality and Testing group will benefit from solid reporting of bugs, allowing them to react to real bugs, versus fixes that exist already.

Remember the words of Edmund Burke which opened this chapter—

"All you have to do is nothing for evil to triumph".

Incident reporting—Why?

As I wrote this section, I noted that another round of attacks has occurred on Joomla!™-based sites. The site administrators come to the Joomla!™ forum for assistance and of course, they must provide more information than "help my site is down and I've been attacked."

While Joomla!™ continues to gain steam in the marketplace, the amount of attacks seems to be rising, a good sign of the spread of Joomla!™. Yet the community must come to the table with more information to help the core team, Quality and Testing team and the support forum membership to address problems, stop these digital terrorists and keep our sites up and running.

By using this form it will give you a process to gather, collate, document, post and archive problems, and solutions. Once you complete this form submit the information to the appropriate forum on Joomla.org. The form **JMS-1000-A** is a multi-part form, and is modeled after the Quality and Testing template from the forums. This form takes into account the needed elements of the Q&T reporting template.

Field:	Purpose:	Required
1.	Describe the bug or problem in detail	YES
2.	Describe the affected function	YES
3.	How can this be replicated? Include steps.	YES
4.	If you have a proposed code fix, include.	NO
5.	Include Version information	YES
6.	Hosting information	NO
7.	Do you have a current backup?	NO
8.	Are your file permissions set correctly?	NO
9.	Enter any cross reference info from Forum	YES
10.	List any related files that may be part of it	YES
11.	List components, modules, mambots/plugins	YES
12.	Joomla!™ System information	YES

It is a good idea to keep a written copy in your maintenance book of this form after submission.

Request for support form: Use to gather information to request help or report bugs

1—mandatory field to report to Q&T

Description: Please describe the bug in your own words with as much detail as possible.

2—mandatory field to report to Q&T

Affected functions: Describe the portions that are affected by this bug.

3—mandatory field to report to Q&T

Steps to replicate: Give a step by step how to replicate the problem.
Provide a live URL for review by Q&T

4—mandatory field to report to Q&T

Proposed fix (if any): List any possible fixes in code that you might have

Document Number: JMSF-1000-A Page 1 of 2

Request for support form: Use to gather information to request help or report bugs

5—mandatory field to report to Q&T

Version info: Joomla!™: ____   Build: ____   PHP: ___   MySql: ___   Apache: ____

6—What type of hosting do you have:

Shared_____   Dedicated _____   Self-host _____   Access to server logs? _____

7—Do you have a backup of SITE (files): _____   Database _____

8—mandatory field to report to Q&T

Topic ID/Artifact ID: Provide the cross reference for the topic or artifact ID/URL:

_____

9—mandatory field to report to Q&T—List related files when known:

10—List of 3rd party extensions installed:

Extension name: *   Extension Version info**

DO NOT INCLUDE:

- **ANY scripts or code that could be used for compromising other sites.**
- **Your passwords, user ID's or any other information that could be exploited such as your IP address**

Admin Focus: Bug reporting how to by Simon Tatham

<u>**Proper reporting of bugs and issues.**</u>[1]

In the next few pages, is an article by Simon Tatham about how to properly report bugs and issues. I have chosen to include this next section because of how much sense it actually makes. I strongly encourage you to adjust your reporting to the community based on this article.

**Special thank to Simon Tatham for his permission to reprint
this great reference in its entirety.**

---

[1]   http://www.chiark.greenend.org.uk/~sgtatham/bugs.html (accessed November 2006)

How to report bugs effectively
by Simon Tatham, professional and free-software programmer

Introduction

Anybody who has written software for public use will probably have received at least one bad bug report. Reports that say nothing ("It doesn't work!"); reports that make no sense; reports that don't give enough information; reports that give wrong information. Reports of problems that turn out to be user error; reports of problems that turn out to be the fault of somebody else's program; reports of problems that turn out to be network failures.

There's a reason why technical support is seen as a horrible job to be in, and that reason is bad bug reports. However, not all bug reports are unpleasant: I maintain free software, when I'm not earning my living, and sometimes I receive wonderfully clear, helpful, informative bug reports.

In this essay I'll try to state clearly what makes a good bug report. Ideally I would like everybody in the world to read this essay before reporting any bugs to anybody. Certainly I would like everybody who reports bugs to me to have read it.

In a nutshell, the aim of a bug report is to enable the programmer to see the program failing in front of them. You can either show them in person, or give them careful and detailed instructions on how to make it fail. If they can make it fail, they will try to gather extra information until they know the cause. If they can't make it fail, they will have to ask you to gather that information for them.

In bug reports, try to make very clear what are actual facts ("I was at the computer and this happened") and what are speculations ("I think the problem might be this"). Leave out speculations if you want to, but don't leave out facts.

When you report a bug, you are doing so because you want the bug fixed. There is no point in swearing at the programmer or being deliberately unhelpful: it may be their fault and your problem, and you might be right to be angry with them, but the bug will get fixed faster if you help them by supplying all the information they need. Remember also that if the program is free, then the author is providing it out of kindness, so if too many people are rude to them then they may stop feeling kind.

This essay is full of guidelines. None of them is an absolute rule. Particular programmers have particular ways they like bugs to be reported. If the program comes with its own set of bug-reporting guidelines, read them. If the guidelines that come with the program contradict the guidelines in this essay, follow the ones that come with the program!

"It doesn't work."

Give the programmer some credit for basic intelligence: if the program really didn't work at all, they would probably have noticed. Since they haven't noticed, it must be working for them. Therefore, either you are doing something differently from them, or your environment is different from theirs. They need information; providing this information is the purpose of a bug report. More information is almost always better than less.

Many programs, particularly free ones, publish their list of known bugs. If you can find a list of known bugs, it's worth reading it to see if the bug you've just found is already known or not. If it's already known, it probably isn't worth reporting again, but if you think you have more information than the report in the bug list, you might want to contact the programmer anyway. They might be able to fix the bug more easily if you can give them information they didn't already have. This essay is full of guidelines. None of them is an absolute rule. Particular programmers have particular ways they like bugs to be reported. If the program comes with its own set of bug-reporting guidelines, read them. If the guidelines that come with the program contradict the guidelines in this essay, follow the ones that come with the program!

If you are not reporting a bug but just asking for help using the program, you should state where you have already looked for the answer to your question. ("I looked in chapter 4 and section 5.2 but couldn't find anything that told me if this is possible.") This will let the programmer know where people will expect to find the answer, so they can make the documentation easier to use.

"Show me."

One of the very best ways you can report a bug is by showing it to the programmer. Stand them in front of your computer, fire up their software, and demonstrate the thing that goes wrong. Let them watch you start the machine, watch you run the software, watch how you interact with the software, and watch what the software does in response to your inputs. They know that software like the back of their hand. They know which parts they trust, and they know which parts are likely to have faults. They know intuitively what to watch for. By the time the software does something obviously wrong, they may well have already noticed something subtly wrong earlier which might give them a clue. They can observe everything the computer does during the test run, and they can pick out the important bits for themselves.

This may not be enough. They may decide they need more information, and ask you to show them the same thing again. They may ask you to talk them through the procedure, so that they can reproduce the bug for themselves as many times as they want. They might try varying the procedure a few times, to see whether the problem occurs in only one case or in a family of related cases. If you're unlucky, they may need to sit down for a couple of hours with a set of development tools and really start investigating.

But the most important thing is to have the programmer looking at the computer when it goes wrong. Once they can see the problem happening, they can usually take it from there and start trying to fix it.

"Show me how to show myself."

This is the era of the Internet. This is the era of worldwide communication. This is the era in which I can send my software to somebody in Russia at the touch of a button, and he can send me comments about it just as easily. But if he has a problem with my program, he can't have me standing in front of it while it fails. "Show me" is good when you can, but often you can't.

If you have to report a bug to a programmer who can't be present in person, the aim of the exercise is to enable them to reproduce the problem. You want the programmer to run their own copy of the program, do the same things to it, and make it fail in the same way. When they can see the problem happening in front of their eyes, then they can deal with it.

So tell them exactly what you did. If it's a graphical program, tell them which buttons you pressed and what order you pressed them in. If it's a program you run by typing a command, show them precisely what command you typed. Wherever possible, you should provide a verbatim transcript of the session, showing what commands you typed and what the computer output in response.

Give the programmer all the input you can think of. If the program reads from a file, you will probably need to send a copy of the file. If the program talks to another computer over a network, you probably can't send a copy of that computer, but you can at least say what kind of computer it is, and (if you can) what software is running on it.

"Works for me. So what goes wrong?"

If you give the programmer a long list of inputs and actions, and they fire up their own copy of the program and nothing goes wrong, then you haven't given them enough information. Possibly the fault doesn't show up on every computer; your system and theirs may differ in some way. Possibly you have misunderstood what the program is supposed to do, and you are both looking at exactly the same display but you think it's wrong and they know it's right.

So also describe what happened. Tell them exactly what you saw. Tell them why you think what you saw is wrong; better still, tell them exactly what you expected to see. If you say "and then it went wrong", you have left out some very important information.

If you saw error messages then tell the programmer, carefully and precisely, what they were. They are important! At this stage, the programmer is not trying to fix the problem: they're just trying to find it. They need to know what has gone wrong, and those error messages are the computer's best effort to tell you that. Write the errors down if you have no other easy way to remember them, but it's not worth reporting that the program generated an error unless you can also report what the error message was.

In particular, if the error message has numbers in it, do let the programmer have those numbers. Just because you can't see any meaning in them doesn't mean there isn't any. Numbers contain all kinds of information that can be read by programmers, and they are likely to contain vital clues. Numbers in error messages are there because the computer is too confused to report the error in words, but is doing the best it can to get the important information to you somehow.

At this stage, the programmer is effectively doing detective work. They don't know what's happened, and they can't get close enough to watch it happening for themselves, so they are searching for clues that might give it away. Error messages, incomprehensible strings of numbers, and even unexplained delays are all just as important as fingerprints at the scene of a crime. Keep them!

If you are using Unix, the program may have produced a core dump. Core dumps are a particularly good source of clues, so don't throw them away. On the other hand, most programmers don't like to receive huge core files by e-mail without warning, so ask before mailing one to anybody. Also, be aware that the core file contains a record of the complete state of the program: any "secrets" involved (maybe the program was handling a personal message, or dealing with confidential data) may be contained in the core file.

"So then I tried …"

There are a lot of things you might do when an error or bug comes up. Many of them make the problem worse. A friend of mine at school deleted all her Word documents by mistake, and before calling in any expert help, she tried reinstalling Word, and then she tried running Defrag. Neither of these helped recover her files, and between them they scrambled her disk to the extent that no Undelete program in the world would have been able to recover anything. If she'd only left it alone, she might have had a chance.

Users like this are like a mongoose backed into a corner: with its back to the wall and seeing certain death staring it in the face, it attacks frantically, because doing something has to be better than doing nothing. This is not well adapted to the type of problems computers produce.

Instead of being a mongoose, be an antelope. When an antelope is confronted with something unexpected or frightening, it freezes. It stays absolutely still and tries not to attract any attention, while it stops and thinks and works out the best thing to do. (If antelopes had a technical support line, it would be telephoning it at this point.) Then, once it has decided what the safest thing to do is, it does it.

When something goes wrong, immediately stop doing anything. Don't touch any buttons at all. Look at the screen and notice everything out of the ordinary, and remember it or write it down.
Then perhaps start cautiously pressing "OK" or "Cancel", whichever seems safest. Try to develop a reflex reaction—if a computer does anything unexpected, freeze.

If you manage to get out of the problem, whether by closing down the affected program or by rebooting the computer, a good thing to do is to try to make it happen again. Programmers like problems that they can reproduce more than once. Happy programmers fix bugs faster and more efficiently.

"I think the tachyon modulation must be wrongly polarized."

It isn't only non-programmers who produce bad bug reports. Some of the worst bug reports I've ever seen come from programmers, and even from good programmers.

I worked with another programmer once, who kept finding bugs in his own code and trying to fix them. Every so often he'd hit a bug he couldn't solve, and he'd call me over to help. What's gone wrong?" I'd ask. He would reply by telling me his current opinion of what needed to be fixed.

This worked fine when his current opinion was right. It meant he'd already done half the work and we were able to finish the job together. It was efficient and useful.

But quite often he was wrong. We would work for some time trying to figure out why some particular part of the program was producing incorrect data, and eventually we would discover that it wasn't, that we'd been investigating a perfectly good piece of code for half an hour, and that the actual problem was somewhere else.

I'm sure he wouldn't do that to a doctor. *"Doctor, I need a prescription for Hydroyoyodyne."* People know not to say that to a doctor: you describe the symptoms, the actual discomforts and aches and pains and rashes and fevers, and you let the doctor do the diagnosis of what the problem is and what to do about it. Otherwise the doctor dismisses you as a hypochondriac or crackpot, and quite rightly so.

It's the same with programmers. Providing your own diagnosis might be helpful sometimes, but always state the symptoms. The diagnosis is an optional extra, and not an alternative to giving the symptoms. Equally, sending a modification to the code to fix the problem is a useful addition to a bug report but not an adequate substitute for one.

If a programmer asks you for extra information, don't make it up! Somebody reported a bug to me once, and I asked him to try a command that I knew wouldn't work. The reason I asked him to try it was that I wanted to know which of two different error messages it would give. Knowing which error message came back would give a vital clue. But he didn't actually try it—he just mailed me back and said "No, that won't work". It took me some time to persuade him to try it for real.

Using your intelligence to help the programmer is fine. Even if your deductions are wrong, the programmer should be grateful that you at least tried to make their life easier. But report the symptoms as well, or you may well make their life much more difficult instead.

"That's funny, it did it a moment ago."

Say "intermittent fault" to any programmer and watch their face fall. The easy problems are the ones where performing a simple sequence of actions will cause the failure to occur. The programmer can then repeat those actions under closely observed test conditions and watch what happens in great detail. Too many problems simply don't work that way: there will be programs that fail once a week, or fail once in a blue moon, or never fail when you try them in front of the programmer but always fail when you have a deadline coming up.

Most intermittent faults are not truly intermittent. Most of them have some logic somewhere. Some might occur when the machine is running out of memory, some might occur when another program tries to modify a critical file at the wrong moment, and some might occur only in the first half of every hour! (I've actually seen one of these.)

Also, if you can reproduce the bug but the programmer can't, it could very well be that their computer and your computer are different in some way and this difference is causing the problem. I had a program once whose window curled up into a little ball in the top left corner of the screen, and sat there and sulked. But it only did it on 800×600 screens; it was fine on my 1024×768 monitor.

The programmer will want to know anything you can find out about the problem. Try it on another machine, perhaps. Try it twice or three times and see how often it fails. If it goes wrong when you're doing serious work but not when you're trying to demonstrate it, it might be long running times or large files that make it fall over. Try to remember as much detail as you can about what you were doing to it when it did fall over, and if you see any patterns, mention them. Anything you can provide has to be some help. Even if it's only probabilistic (such as "it tends to crash more often when Emacs is running"), it might not provide direct clues to the cause of the problem, but it might help the programmer reproduce it.

Most importantly, the programmer will want to be sure of whether they're dealing with a true intermittent fault or a machine-specific fault. They will want to know lots of details about your computer, so they can work out how it differs from theirs. A lot of these details will depend on the particular program, but one thing you should definitely be ready to provide is version numbers. The version number of the program itself, and the version number of the operating system, and probably the version numbers of any other programs that are involved in the problem.

"So I loaded the disk on to my Windows ..."

Writing clearly is essential in a bug report. If the programmer can't tell what you meant, you might as well not have said anything.

I get bug reports from all around the world. Many of them are from non-native English speakers, and a lot of those apologize for their poor English. In general, the bug reports with apologies for their poor English are actually very clear and useful. All the most unclear reports come from native English speakers who assume that I will understand them even if they don't make any effort to be clear or precise.

Be specific. If you can do the same thing two different ways, state which one you used. "I selected Load" might mean "I clicked on Load" or "I pressed Alt-L". Say which you did. Sometimes it matters.

Be verbose. Give more information rather than less. If you say too much, the programmer can ignore some of it. If you say too little, they have to come back and ask more questions. One bug report I received was a single sentence; every time I asked for more information, the reporter would reply with another single sentence. It took me several weeks to get a useful amount of information, because it turned up one short sentence at a time.

Be careful of pronouns. Don't use words like "it", or references like "the window", when it's unclear what they mean. Consider this: "I started FooApp. It put up a warning window. I tried to close it and it crashed." It isn't clear what the user tried to close. Did they try to close the warning window, or the whole of FooApp? It makes a difference. Instead, you could say "I started FooApp, which put up a warning window. I tried to close the warning window, and FooApp crashed." This is longer and more repetitive, but also clearer and less easy to misunderstand.

Read what you wrote. Read the report back to yourself, and see if you think it's clear. If you have listed a sequence of actions which should produce the failure, try following them yourself, to see if you missed a step.

Summary

- The first aim of a bug report is to let the programmer see the failure with their own eyes. If you can't be with them to make it fail in front of them, give them detailed instructions so that they can make it fail for themselves.
- In case the first aim doesn't succeed, and the programmer can't see it failing themselves, the second aim of a bug report is to describe what went wrong. Describe everything in detail. State what you saw, and also state what you expected to see. Write down the error messages, especially if they have numbers in.
- When your computer does something unexpected, freeze. Do nothing until you're calm, and don't do anything that you think might be dangerous.
- By all means try to diagnose the fault yourself if you think you can, but if you do, you should still report the symptoms as well.
- Be ready to provide extra information if the programmer needs it. If they didn't need it, they wouldn't be asking for it. They aren't being deliberately awkward. Have version numbers at your fingertips, because they will probably be needed.
- Write clearly. Say what you mean, and make sure it can't be misinterpreted. Above all, be precise. **Programmers like precision.**

Reporting abuse to a ISP/HOST provider

The following is a WHOIS from IANA, the authority who assigns Internet numbers. I chose them because they are generic enough to describe the portions that you need to pay attention to.

This example is meant to show you how to read the WHOIS information. It has been edited down for space reasons in this book.

To obtain this type of information visit www.dnsstuff.com and enter the offending IP address in the WHOIS lookup box on the lower left.

The first part of our example is who the owner of this particular IP block is.

OrgName:	**Internet Assigned Numbers Authority**
OrgID:	**IANA**
Address:	**4676 Admiralty Way, Suite 330**
City:	**Marina del Rey**
StateProv:	**CA**
PostalCode:	**90292–6695**
Country:	**US**

The NetRange will show if the offending IP address falls into their *netblock*.

NetRange:	**192.168.0.0—192.168.255.255**
CIDR:	**192.168.0.0/16**
NetName:	**IANA-CBLK1**
NetHandle:	**NET-192–168–0-0–1**
Parent:	**NET-192–0-0–0-0**

To report review this part as it is very important—all complaints against an offender can be directed to the ORGABUSE e-mail or ORGABUSE phone number

OrgAbuseName:	**Internet Corporation for Assigned Names and Number**
OrgAbusePhone:	**+1–310–301–5820**
OrgAbuseEmail:	*****@iana.org**

It is wise to report, with a polite (no cursing, threats, abusive language) e-mail to the appropriate party. Include in your report details from your logs such as time, specific attack vectors (how they attacked you), the IP address or addresses in question. If a handle or name is available enclose that. Be sure and include proper contact information for yourself and close politely with them telling them that you would be happy to provide further information should they need it.

Once you have reported it, get back to recovering your site. If it is a large attack from a specific net block, feel free to block that range using .htaccess for a time. Many crackers will get bored and move on. If you are attacked by a foreign telecom/ISP IP address and you will never worry about doing anything with those Countries citizens, then block the entire range. This at a minimum will keep you from being attacked from there, and could easily lower your bandwidth consumption. *That is not to say you won't be attacked from a different ISP however.*

Closing words

Stop reading if you've heard this one!

Patient: "Doc it hurts when I move my arm like this—what can I do?"

Doc: "Don't move it!"

Yes, it is an old joke and not a very good one; however, this typifies why technical support generally gets a bad grade from the public.

The person reporting to the support number or forum most of the time does not include enough information about the problem to achieve resolution. They may or may not understand why they have to give more information than they thought. As the frustration on the part of the user and the supporting person rises, the ultimate answer "did you RTM? (aka: *read the manual*)" often is the response. Usually once you get that response you're sunk and you must regroup (I.E. RTM) to get a response.

This chapter covered the method to collect and report to the community and the Q&T team. It is written taking into account the current method that the Q&T has requested you report problems.

In addition to reporting to Joomla!™, you were introduced to a method of reporting attacks to your ISP or Host about where the attack appeared to originate from.

If you want help then by all means help yourself before reporting by reading the forums, searching to see if others have had the same problem. You might be surprised what you find.

If you however have been diligent in searching, then report the problem, and follow the forms in this chapter. You will be viewed as professional, structured, and likely will get immediate help. If you have encountered real bug, the use of these forms will help the Q&T group duplicate it, and get it fixed, thus helping the rest of the community.

Topics covered in this chapter

- **Reporting methods and means for success**
- **Methods to track changes and updates**
- **An excellent white paper on reporting errors**

Chapter 6

Plan of Action

"Being prepared IS job 1"

Why you should read this chapter

Disaster—the meaning of it has its root in early Italian,
from the word disastro (Meaning away from star).

It was thought that an unfavorable position of a star or planet was the
cause of mishaps and calamities[1]

Disaster preparedness is what you do before, not after, a disaster hits. Crackers/hackers are only part of your concern.

What about weather events such as Hurricane Katrina?

What about terrorist acts such as 9/11?

What about a *disgruntled* employee or simply fire, or hardware failure?

Depending on the level of problem or disaster, you will need to respond
in a process oriented way.

Learning goals in this chapter

- A working plan that you designed for your businesses web site
- Full understanding of the four components to a disaster preparedness plan

1. **Document your business**
2. **Determine risks**
3. **Build your plan**
4. **Test and document**

---

[1]   Robert K. Barnhart, "The Barnhart concise Dictionary of Etymology—The origins of American English words", (New York: HarperCollins books, 1995) 208

Plan of Action

You control a large group the same as you control a few
You divide their ranks correctly
You fight a large army the same as you fight a small one
You only need the right position and communication
You may meet a large enemy army.
You must be able to sustain an enemy attack without being defeated

Sun Tzu—The Art of War

*T*he goal of this chapter is to help you prepare your to business keep on running after a disaster. For our purposes, your disaster preparedness plan (DP) plan is a set of processes that defines a strategic and tactical plan to recover from a disaster to your site. It doesn't matter where that disaster comes from, it only matters you are prepared to act; not just 'react'.

A disaster is anything that causes your IT systems to stop or fail. Be that a backhoe cutting your ISP's lines or a cracker attacking your site, fire in your datacenter or a flood.

Why is this chapter so important? If you are a business of ANY SIZE a 1978 study by the University of Minnesota states that a business can only survive an interruption of two to six days in length.[2] Given the Internet has *compressed time* for us, I would say that length of time might be even shorter. There is always someone there to take your place in line on the Internet.

I want you, the reader, to take this chapter to heart, apply what is within it to your business website to ensure your surviability This chapter will take you through a series of learnings and some exercises, data gathering, and thinking; all planned to help you create your own response plan.

Please visit our site at www.joomspyder.com to download the entire set of forms.

---

[2]   Aasgaard, D.O. et al., "An evaluation of Data processing 'Machine room' Loss and Selected Recovery Strategies," MISRC Working Papers (Minneapolis, MN: University of Minnesota, 1978)

Disaster Preparedness Plan

Emergency restoration procedures are the heart of your disaster preparedness plan. It is one thing to have them; it is another to know how to use them. Ideally, you want the plan to be clear enough that anyone familiar with your setup could step in and take care of your sites unique needs.

The forms in this chapter are designed to capture the information you need to commence a restoration following a disaster. They contain highly sensitive information and must be kept in a safe place. They must never be stored "on-line" or on any magnetic media. If you wish to keep a copy on a USB memory key, ensure that the key is only a backup to the paper version and is secured by password as well as being physically secured.

Your disaster preparedness plan is a living, breathing document. You will as part of your plan need to review and update this on a regularly scheduled basis. Use these forms in this book as scratch or practice. Use them to gather the requirements, contact information and other important facts. When you are done you will find a full set of forms located in the back of this book, to create your own set.

You may also visit our website and download the entire forms package. These forms may be updated occasionally so be sure and check from time to time to download the latest.

On our site in addition to being able to download the entire form package, we offer a fee based service on www.joomspyder.com to order forms and binders customized to your site. You can see an example at www.joomspyder.com. Please visit our site for further information.

Admin Focus: Things to consider as you plan[3]

These represent some things to consider as you work through this planning and documentation. We have weaved into this book in various sections portions of this.

- Carefully assess **how your company functions**, both internally and externally, to determine which staff, materials, procedures and equipment are absolutely necessary to keep the business operating.
- Identify **operations critical to survival** and recovery.
- Include **emergency payroll, expedited financial decision-making and accounting systems** to track and document costs in the event of a disaster.
- Establish procedures for **succession of management**. Include at least one person who is not at the company headquarters, if applicable.
- Identify your **suppliers, shippers, resources and other businesses** you must interact with on a daily basis.
- Develop **professional relationships** with **more than one** company to use in case your primary contractor cannot service your needs. A disaster that shuts down a key supplier can be devastating to your business.
- Plan with your suppliers, shippers and others you regularly do business with.
- **Create a contact list** for existing critical business contractors and others you plan to use in an emergency. Keep this list with other important documents on file, in your **emergency supply kit** and at an off-site location.
- Plan what you will do if your home, building, plant or store is not accessible.
- Plan what you will do if your **home, building, plant or store is not accessible**.
- Consider if you can run the business from a **different location** or from your home.
- **Develop relationships** with other companies to use their facilities in case a disaster makes your location unusable.
- **Plan for payroll continuity**.—how will you pay employees?
- Decide **who should participate** in putting together your emergency plan.—if you are more than 1 person in your company you should pick the person(s) in charge of various functions.
- Include co-workers from all levels in planning and as **active members** of the emergency management team.
- Consider a **broad cross-section** of people from throughout your organization, but focus on those with expertise vital to daily **business functions**. These will likely include people with technical skills as well as managers and executives.
- Make sure those involved **know** what they are supposed to do.
- Train others in case you need back-up help.
- **Plan** with your suppliers, shippers and others you regularly do business with.

---

[3]   http://www.ready.gov/business/plan/planning.html (December 2006)

Developing your disaster preparedness plan.

Your disaster preparedness plan is only as good as the data you provide. Having a solid response plan allows you to respond, not out of a *reactionary* mode, but rather a planned response helping to keep the level of panic in check.

The components of your response plan are as follows:

1.   Executive Summary.

This section lay's out a very high level view of your site, your business, its function and the specific security measures in place. It is a summary of how you will respond to a disaster.

It is important to take the time to craft your executive summary even if it is two paragraphs and you only sell cocktail napkins.

2. Contacts, inventory and login/Passcode information.

In this section you will fill out very specific information about the software configurations, passwords, forum URL's, local information, etc., that pertains to you.

3.   Instructions in initiating the disaster preparedness plan

Having a process means, you have to know when the process commences.

4. Identify the critical resources that will be needed
   People, money, materials, vehicles, software, hardware, etc

5. Keep your disaster preparedness plan up to date
   Schedule reviews after any major change

Your plan is important because you, your site and your stake holders are important.

1. Executive Summary (sample only)

At **widgetworldwebsite.com** we are the number one provider to United States and Canada for Widgets. We do one-hundred percent of our sales through our online portal located at **www.widgetworldwebsite.com**. Due to this our sales portal must be operational one-hundred percent of the time with no room for downtime. We are co-located at Bob's house of Hosting, they offer twenty-four hour round the clock support and hands on staff for hardware issues. Their data center is a secure facility with redundant power as well as five major ISP's coming into the site. They conduct LOCAL tape backups on site which are then removed nightly and taken off site.

The host is running the latest in state-of-the art firewall load balancing system. Their building is protected from fire with a Dry Pipe System minimizing any damage to the datacenter and systems. The facility is protected from a power outage with an onsite generator and UPS, with seventy-two hours of fuel on site and fuel contracts to replenish that.

Our specific equipment is protected by an additional UPS local to our systems.

Since **widgetworldwebsite.com** receives orders from all over the world, we have a policy to be up and able to accept orders 24X7X365.

Our business needs dictate we have a second data center and be operational on it within two hours should the need arise.

We do a daily database dump every night at 21:00 automatically from our MySql database and it is stored off site as well.

###

Widgetworldwebsite.com sounds like a major operation doesn't it? The reality is this executive summary was modeled after a two man shop. In essence this executive summary is modeled from a real company who has those real needs.

As part of your DP plan you need to write out a 1 or 2 paragraph Executive Summary about your business or site. Write it as if you were presenting this to a high level CEO of a large company and you wanted him or her to have a good understanding of your business and how you intend to accomplish recovery in the face of a disaster.

<u>Put yourself in the mindset of a Fortune 100 Executive. What would you write?</u>

Writing your executive summary

It is to be kept short and concise, reducing where possible highly technical terms

The DP plan is important to give direction during a crisis. The executive summary is the capstone of that plan.

Note the words of Sun Tzu regarding planning and leadership:

*If the army is confused and suspicious, the neighboring states will surely cause trouble. This is like saying: "**A confused army provides victory for the enemy**"* [4]

The form that follows provides you a general outline to help you get started. There are many good books on the subject of writing executive summaries. Visit www.joomspyder.com to learn more.

Since your plan is considered confidential, you will not be speaking to an outside audience, but rather an internal one. Thus there is no need to 'sell' your plan to the reader. The plan is an operational order to your staff. They do not have the luxury of not *investing* in the plan.

On the next page, you will be given a form to help you collect your thoughts on very important points and document them. This again is not meant to be the final written form. Rather you will create the final written form based on what you put down here.

---

[4]   Hou, Wee Chow, et. al., "Sun Tzu—War and Management", (Addison-Wesley, 1991) 27

Executive summary planning form   **Page 1 of 2**

Business Name: _____

    Address One: _____

    Address Two: _____

City, St, Zip or Postal code: _____

Telephone: _____ **Fax:** _____

Website Address: _____

List items that you feel will make your business or web site succeed

-
-
-
-
-
-
-
-
-
-
-
-
-
-
-
-
-

Out of the above list, note the items you consider THE most important

-
-
-
-
-
-
-

Executive summary planning form   **Page 2 of 2**

List important parts of your DP that apply to your scenario

-
-
-
-
-
-
-
-
-
-
-

Write out your executive summary below, using the points you gathered.

2.   Contacts, inventory and login/Passcode information.

In the next several pages you will gather the necessary information about:

- **Contacts: emergency and non-emergency**
- **Support Forums**
- **Site inventory forms covering components, mambots, plugins, modules, code to include (such as specialized template code), code to NOT include after restoration.**

These forms are designed to help you in the event of a total loss of your site, allowing you the admin to quickly recreate the site.

The telephone forms are built with the idea of 'alerting' your staff, management, customers and more.

Emergency Contact Form

Site URL: http://_____

Site URL: https://_____

My technical Support Contacts:

HOST:( ) ___—____   Account Number _____   Other _____

ISP: ( ) ___—____   Account Number _____ Other _____

HOST ABUSE E-mail: _____ ISP ABUSE E-mail: _____

Passcode/Passwords:

Host _____   Database _____

Super Admin USER _____ Super Admin Password _____

Server Password _____Control panel/Plesk Password _____

FTP User _____   FTP Password _____

Other user id _____

Other passwords _____

What is this for? _____

Security Verification Information: Generic

What is this for? _____

Credentials _____

Any other information: _____

Emergency Contact form—Other

Name	Telephone	Cell phone	Text/SMS/Pager

Support URLS & My Forums

These should be support forums pertaining to YOUR specific site. If some component/mod does not have a forum, list the authors e-mail or an alternate location to seek help

STAY UP TO SPEED ON JOOMLA!™ ANNOUCEMENTS
HTTP://FORUM.JOOMLA .ORG/INDEX.PHP?ACTION=NOTIFYBOARD;BOARD=8.0

FORUM NAME	FORUM URL	user/password

Document number: SUMF-1000-A

Site Inventory: **URL:** _____
Components

Joomla!™ Version   V_____   Patch Level _____
Minimum version 1.0.12

Component	Author	Version	Date	E-mail	Author
Example					
URL Banners	Joomla!™	1.0.0	July 2004		admin@Joomla.org

_____

_____

_____

_____

_____

_____

_____

_____

_____

_____

_____

_____

_____

_____

_____

_____

_____

_____

_____

_____

_____

_____

_____

_____

Document number: ICOM-1000-A

Site Inventory: **URL:** _____
Modules

Joomla!™ Version   V_____   Patch Level _____
Minimum version 1.0.12

Component	Author	Version	Date	E-mail	Author
Example					
URL Banners	Joomla!™	1.0.0	July 2004		admin@Joomla.org

_____

_____

_____

_____

_____

_____

_____

_____

_____

_____

_____

_____

_____

_____

_____

_____

_____

_____

_____

Document number: IMOD-1000-A

Site Inventory: **URL:** _____
Plugins/Mambots

Joomla!™ Version   V_____ Patch Level _____
Minimum version 1.0.12

Component	Author	Version	Date	E-mail	Author
Example					
URL Banners	Joomla!™	1.0.0	July 2004		admin@Joomla.org

Site Inventory: **SITE URL:** _____
Specialized code

Code Snip, location, purpose

Example
CODE:

```php
<?php

if (file_exists($mosConfig_absolute_path."/components/com_ebackup/ebackup.php")){

echo "<img src=\"".$mosConfig_live_site."/index2.php?option=com_ebackup\" width=\"0\" height=\"0\" alt=\"\"/>\n";
}
?>
```

Location: Installed in SITE TEMPLATE HTML

Purpose: This is required to run the ebackup utility

Code:

Location: _____

Purpose: _____

Code:

Location: _____

Purpose: _____

Document Number: SPCI-1000-A

Site Inventory: **SITE URL:** _____
Banned Code

Banned Code Snip, location and reason it was banned.

Code:

<bad code sample>

Location: Installed in SITE TEMPLATE HTML

Purpose: Causes the template to move to the right _____

Code:

Location: _____

Purpose: _____

Code:

Location: _____

Purpose: _____

Document number: BC-1000-A

3. Initiating the disaster preparedness plan

This form helps you capture the finite detail of who can and should initiate a plan and why.

WHO:

- **Determines if a action needs to be taken**
- **Will activate the plan**

Instructions:

Question one:

In this question you will detail what peril will make you break out your plan and activate it. There are clearly more reasons than are listed. If you don't find your choice, write it out in the section labeled: *Other*

What warrants a disaster?

- **Site down for 30 minutes or more?**
- **Data center flood?**
- **Attack by digital terrorists/crackers?**
- **Phone lines cut?**
- **Hardware failure**

Question two:

Giving someone the responsibility to activate the plan is a big step in protecting your organization if you were not available. List the people you, including yourself, who can activate the plan.

Page two of the form

There could be other information that is beyond the scope of this form, such as UPS start up procedures, alarm codes or the combination to the fireproof safe. This section is for you to detail out information that doesn't fit anywhere else.

Plan Initiation   URL: _____

Question one:

Outage: Site is unreachable or cannot be pinged by multiple computers or clearly is not working.

How long before you initiate your DR plan?

**Reason to initiate plan
(Not time dependant)**

30 min ___

Defacement ___

1 hour ___

DOS Attack ___

1/2 Day ___

Scheduled Outage ___

1 Day ___

Other: Please define below:

OTHER OUTAGE REASON:

_____

Question Two:

List of staff or persons who can activate the plan:

Name	Telephone	Cell/Mobile	Text/SMS

Document Number: PIF-1000-A

Plan Initiation   URL: _____

Information needed such as building codes, key locations, alarm settings, etc.

Alarm codes: _____

Key location: _____

Security monitoring password: _____

Special instructions for other security functions:

Combination to parts locker, vault, etc: _____

Completing Emergency Restoration Procedures form—3rd party hosted

If you are not making your own backups you will need to ensure your host is backing up and that you know how to request a restoration. While no two hosts will be alike, this form has been designed to capture the information from just about any host and record it.

Field	Description
• URL	What site URL does this plan cover?
• Support number/option	Number and options you need to select
• Technical account manager	If you are assigned a TAM record it here
• Restoration costs/time	List fees for restoration and time required
• Backup frequency	How often do they conduct full backups?
• Host current procedure	Is it tape? Disk to disk? Is it offsite?
• Security fields	List all appropriate security information
• Authorized user fields	This is who can authorize a restore
• Confirmation site is up	Post restore check to verify site is up
• Sign off	Responsible parties in your chain of Command that need to sign off for future reference and archival.

Take the time to contact your host and gather all this information. It is a good practice to recertify this information regularly. I suggest that you take the time to do so before a mock-drill.

Don't forget to keep all your documentation up after you check for changes.

Emergency Restoration Procedures—Hosted pg 1 of 2   URL:

Support phone number: (   )   -   **Extension or option number:** _____

Restoration costs ($$$): _____   what is the restoration time?   _____ (hrs/mins)

HOSTING ONLY: How often does your host backup?
Nightly ____ Weekly _____ Monthly _____ Never _____

Hosts current procedure for backing up:

Security information I will need to give host to initiate restoration

Account number: _____   Password or Passcode: _____

Other: _____   Other: _____

Who can initiate the restoration?

First approval contact name: _____ Num: (   ) ____-_____

Second approval contact name: _____ Num: (   ) ____-_____

Other important information for restoration

Signature of primary approver   _____

Name of primary approver   _____

Signature of secondary approver _____

Name of secondary approver   _____

Emergency Restoration Procedures—Hosted pg 2 of 2   Site URL: _____

Confirmation that site is backup and functional _____

REQUIRED: Check site for malicious scripts, wrong revision code and other items that may cause site to incur further downtime or issues   Answer (y/n) ____

Scripts _____   Down Revision _____

Correct template _____   Custom code back in place _____

Signature of primary approver   _____

Name of primary approver   _____

Signature of secondary approver   _____

Name of secondary approver   _____

Document number ERP3P-1000-A

Retrieving backup media from offsite locations

Instructions for retrieving the offsite backup media

When the time comes to retrieve your backup media, it may be as close as a fireproof safe or might be located at your host. The retrieval form is designed to record how and where to retrieve the media from.

Field	Description
Media Storage Information	Specific information about where the backup media is stored.
Facility access information	Time/days, telephone, authorized users
What type of media?	Use this to identify media being retrieved
Special handling needs	If media has special needs for transport list them here.
What is media labeled?	List the name of the media

Backup media offsite storage   Site URL: _____

Part One: **Address, contact, Hours**

Address where the backup media is stored:

_____

_____

Name of company: _____   Telephone: _____ X_____

Contact 1: _____   Contact 2: _____

Location attributes: (y/n)

Water proof? ____   Fire proof/protected? ____   Static guarded: ____   Secure? ___ Open 24/7 ____

If facility is not open 24/7, what days/times is it open? Days_____ Times _____

Security information to drop off or pick up backup media.

Account/Auth num/._____   Passcode/Security Code _____

Authorized users	**Telephone #**	**Interaction allowed (y/n)**	**DR start up allowed (y/n)**
_____	_____	_____	_____
_____	_____	_____	_____
_____	_____	_____	_____

Part Two: **What type of media will you be storing**

Tape: **Hard media ___**   **Other media _____**

Dat: _____   CD   ___   USB drive/Media: Size: _____
DLT ____   DVD   ___   Secured (y/n)   _____
DDS ____   Removable ___   Passcode: _____
Other _____ Type: _____

List special handling needs for media/Labeling standards for media

Document number—OSS-1000-A

4.   Identify the critical resources that will be needed

As you are preparing your plan consider what non-technical (i.e. not software or applications) items you will need. To get you thinking I have included a non-exhaustive list of items to consider that you *may* need to have on hand to deal with a disaster event. Again this list does not represent a shopping list but is meant to give you an idea of developing *your own* DR responder kit.

- Staff
- Emergency power
- Water
- Blankets/cots
- Cars with a predefined egress plan
- Restoration media (tape, cd, hard drive, etc …)
- Your DR Handbook
- Flashlights
- Non-perishable or long shelf life food
- Cash
- Fuel for automobiles
- If you are on a building generator have you confirmed emergency fuel supplies?
- Road maps
- Hotel/Motel telephone numbers

While you may never need this list of items it only makes good sense to think through scenario's based on your particular situation.

In your planning consider if you were stuck in recovery mode for an extended period due to weather. If the building power fails and it were winter will you be able to stay warm?

The entire point of this step is to help you think through the various scenarios you may face and possible solutions to them before they become a contributing factor.

Note: This is not a comprehensive guide to protecting your facility or your personnel. That is beyond the scope of this book. For that I suggest reading the two books listed in chapter 1.

5. Keep your disaster preparedness plan up to date

Part of keeping your plan up to date is to integrate changes into your routine and plan.

Things you want to keep a close eye out for are:

- Did phone numbers or contacts change?
- Is the URL and Forum website addresses correct?
- Did the testing uncover any miswritten information?
- Does the plan work for you? Can it be reordered
- Are the instructions clearly written so that they can be followed?

While there are a number of other stumbling blocks to success, these are some that in my experience are the most common.

As part of your test, update your documentation, collect the old documentation and distribute new documentation, based on the results of the test.

Plan maintenance
To be effective, the plan must be maintained in a ready state that accurately reflects system requirements, procedures, organizational structure, and policies. IT systems [and web sites, web applications] undergo frequent changes because of shifting business needs, technology upgrades, new internal or external policies. As part of your change management process you should review, and update this plan on a regular basis. As a general rule, the plan should be reviewed for accuracy, and completeness at least bi-annually or whenever significant changes occur to any element of the site. Certain elements will require more frequent reviews, such as contact lists. Based on the system type and criticality, it may be reasonable to evaluate plan contents and procedures more frequently. At a minimum, plan reviews should focus on the following elements:

- **Operational requirements—does the plan still work?**
- **Security requirements—have you kept up with the latest in security problems?**
- **Technical procedures—for instance has a new backup tool been implemented?**
- **Hardware, software, and other equipment (types, specifications, and amount)**
- **Names and contact information of team members**
- **Names and contact information of vendors including alternate points of contact**
- **Alternate and offsite facility requirements**
- **Vital records (electronic and hardcopy).**

Your disaster preparedness plan contains sensitive operational and personal information. The books should be marked and controlled and distributed to key employees only. You should keep an offsite copy in a safe place in the event you lose or otherwise cannot reach the plan.

Closing words

As this chapter closes, you have been introduced to a strategy to reduce the chances data of loss due to a genuine disaster. In the event of a disaster you must be able to minimize the impact to your critical business functions.

One point of consideration I want to leave you with is, that if the gathering of the information proved to be difficult for what ever reason, imagine what it will be like to conduct a restore or respond to a crisis, without this information.

As the end of this book is near, you will be able to test your processes and forms.

Be sure you complete them before conducting any disaster test.

Topics covered in this chapter

- **Where your weaknesses are knowledge wise**
- **Where your strengths are knowledge wise**
- **A solid inventory of your site or sites**
- **How your host conducts a restoration**
- **A nearly working site disaster preparedness plan**

Chapter 7

Conducting a mock up drill

The difference between success and disaster is training

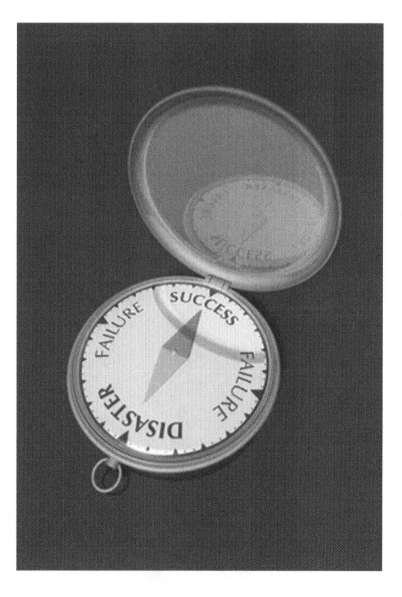

Why read this chapter

The purpose of testing your preparation plan is to find holes, and ensure all the parties involved know what to do if disaster strikes.

Remember your plan is very likely to fail the first few times through.
Take these opportunities to refine your processes.

Learning goals for this chapter

- How to setup a drill
- Roles and responsibilities of each player
- Defining the purpose of your test
- Taking notes
- Change management

Governing a large number as though
Governing a small number is a matter of
Division into groups.
Battling a large number as though
Battling a small number is a matter
Of forms and calls

Sun Tzu—Strategic Advance

C onducting drills will help you flesh out the plan ensuring you haven't missed anything. It will point out problems with your planning. It will help your staff (even if that's just you) learn the procedures needed to recover and respond.

I highly recommend you drill two times a year. This gives you four months to plan, document, and write test scenarios. And about one month to cover the loose ends, train staff, and of course the month to conduct testing. The plan exists in paper and must exist in the minds of you and your staff. They have to mentally own it.

One other point that you personally must bear in mind is your plan *will fail* the first time through; be aware but don't be discouraged.

In this chapter you will be asked to identify team member roles and responsibilities. This is a great place to assign your internal point of contact and your neutral observer. If you work closely with a vendor such as a hardware or software vendor you can integrate them into the testing.

I cannot stress the importance of communication with your team. And again if your team is only two people make sure you're talking. If you have a larger staff, I would suggest that you take your direct report lead and work closely with them to develop the scenarios. I would not use the entire team to develop the scenarios. After they are developed however make sure you run it past them for a reality check.

On the day of the test make sure everyone has a copy of the plan in advance. Get some coffee, juice, pastries, etc. This will stave off hunger helping them stay focused on the task at hand.

After the test, collect all notes, and confirm you're debriefing within one week. Do not wait any longer because memories tend to start fading, rather use this debrief to coach, improve, and document changes for the next test.

Again remember that your plan will fail the first time you go through it. It might fail the second time, and so on. Keep at it because each failure leads you to a successful plan.

Education of your team

If you have a staff be prepared they most likely will not buy off on the idea of a disaster plan, and may possibly resist any effort to train on the plan. This is to be expected, and not taken personally. Being a trainer in my career for several years, I can tell you that students will respond most favorably if the class is prepared, concise and structured. This includes giving them a set of goals that they can expect to achieve.

- **Get to the point.** Nothing bores students more when attending a training class, especially a technical one that has two hours of preamble. Remember to not go down rat holes such as *that's not the way I would do it*. It's your plan, take the input, but you make the decision of the strategy to accomplish a solid disaster preparedness plan.
- **Establish an agenda and keep to it**. This means establishing the time you will spend on the subject. For instance if you were training on **phpmyadmin** to do a restoration, your course agenda, and materials should reflect this. Going down a rabbit hole of "what-if" is not appropriate and only serves to destroy what you are trying to accomplish.

Your training should prepare the staff using the following means

- Formal hands on training with the technologies involved.
- Distribution of the preparedness plan that they will be involved in. For the purposes of Joomla!™-based sites I recommend the entire disaster preparedness book that you will construct out of this. You need to make the judgment call about distribution of sensitive information such as backup media retrieval or phone numbers of executives, customers and so on.
- Dress rehearsal is where you activate the plan in a test scenario, and judge the response of your staff, the accuracy of the plan you wrote, and if it met your time frame. This is probably best done as a paper exercise.
- After action report (AKA Post mortem) after the dress rehearsal. The staff should bring their ideas and thoughts forward in their various expertise areas at this point.

Maintaining your plan

Establishing a formal change management procedure will help to ensure your plan is always as up to date as possible. For example if a new version of *ebackup* is introduced or if you change to another backup method you will need to document, and test this in a mock drill. Change to your documentation, and processes is best handled through a change control method that documents the changes, and assignment of responsibilities for distribution of the new procedures to all involved.

Part of your process should be to establish a schedule for review of the plan.
Other means of change may very well come from an actual crisis.

Admin Focus: Change management—what is it? Why is it important?

Change management is making sure that the people are doing the right things at the right time, *and documenting it!* This includes the downstream and upstream impacts to your organization this may have to the business and operations of your company. Using good change management you can avoid downtime.

The entire subject of change management is beyond the scope of this book; however I think a few good things to touch on are as follows:

Yourself

This is always considered in the first person, no matter who you are. How well do you know yourself? How open to criticism are you? If change is expected and needed are you the type of person who embraces change or do you flee in fear from it? The answers only matter to you, but the resulting actions from them will impact positively or negatively your business.

Your staff

When addressing change with your team, you as the leader need to establish up front how change will be conceived, and documented changes are implemented. There are lots of tools available to help you with this. Other factors include the team knowing themselves as well. When your team approaches a major upgrade, everyone needs to know what the plan is and who is doing what. During a disaster or mock-drill having a 'systemized' plan in place will only make things smoother.

Your business

Also known as 'the big picture' is a complex collection of systems, processes, and people which includes your customers, stake holders, and users. How will your changes affect them? What will happen upstream (your stakeholders, supporting members, vendors) and downstream (users, customers, etc). If your host were to make a sweeping change what would the downstream effect to you be? None of the questions are easy.

For further reading and a very good perspective on change management I would suggest visiting the following website for a complete training package on change management:

http://www.change-management-toolbook.com

Paper testing vs. live testing

In your mock scenarios, it is a wise plan to conduct a 'paper' test at least two or three times to ensure you have everything documented properly.

A scenario of that nature would look like this:

Role Assignments

Who can activate the plan   _____

Who has responsibilities to retrieve backup media   _____

Person(s) responsible for recreation of database on host   _____

Who is the note taker: _____

Who is the primary person to funnel information for dissemination _____

Conducting test

Each person will 'act' out their roles with the team. While in the paper-test mode, no one will actually gather media or reconstruct the databases. The purpose of this is for each person to talk out their actions. Going through the books together, noting that it is done. This will not test any real world problems such as a database that for some reason cannot be recreated, however this will eliminate any procedural issues such as improper documentation.

I highly recommend you purchase and read the this book before you conduct your paper drill:

E-Myth Revisited—Michael Gerber
ISBN: 0887307280

You can find this at Amazon.com, Barnesandnobles.com or practically any bookstore.

The rest of this chapter will focus on the live testing aspect of your mock drill.

Putting your plan to the test—Dress rehearsal

You have prepared your materials, backed up your site, filled out your forms and you are ready to start the mock test.

The first item you need to prepare is yourself. You as the leader of the test must remain calm and assertive during the entire test. Do not lose your cool because those involved are looking to you to lead them and stay steady. With that in mind let's cover the proper mock drill method.

What is it you're testing? You may be thinking—the disaster plan of course! Part of a successful test is determining 'what' you want to accomplish. Do you want to test restore? Do you want to test backup? Do you want to simulate a site failure? Do you want to test upgrading the core?

Deciding this will help you to frame up a successful test. Defining the success metrics will give you the knowledge your test and plan were successful.

When is your test? Consider when the best time will be to do your test. If this is a restoration test to a development site then anytime is fine. If you want to test your live site make every attempt to plan this when the least impact to your site will be. Other considerations are technical support. If you need support will someone be available?

Who is responsible for what parts of the test? Defining roles and responsibility keeps everyone from stepping on each other. If you have more than one person in the test you need to assign roles.

Where will the test be conducted? If you are hosting your own server, then chances are you will hold it at your data center. However if you are more than likely not hosting, you need to decide in advance where to meet, what time to meet and who should be present. If you're staff knows where they are assigned then you will not spend time chasing down people, and wasting time that during a disaster would hurt your recovery time.

How do you prepare materially for the test? Food comes to mind, it helps keep people feeling up and not thinking about hunger. What about your backup media? What about your DP books? Think through what materially you will need.

Have you notified management and stakeholders of testing? This group should play an integral part of your test. In fact if they do not, you may not have the support you need to fund or conduct future drills.

Planning and execution of mock drill—example

Purpose of test: restoration test of www.widgetworldwebsite.com

Date: May 7, 2007, 8:30 am
Items needed:

- **DP Books**
- **Current backup conducted before test**
- **Backup media to restore**
- **Roles assigned**
- **Notify management and stakeholders of test**

Description of test: This test will be to simulate a complete failure of www.widgetworldwebsite.com. It will be conducted on a test domain of our sandbox site located at URL: www.widgetworldwebsite22.com. We will begin the test by activating our disaster preparedness plan stating a complete loss of our website.

Success metrics

- Show a return to operations within 2 hours after failure notification
- Successful retrieval of backup media within 30 minutes of alert
- Complete positive notification to management and stakeholders of 'site-failure'
- Updated status to team and management every 15 minutes of progress
- Testing of operations of site—ensuring all functions back up and running.
- Notification to management and stakeholders of test success or failure

After action report

Within two days following the test the team will gather and review how well the test went. The note taker shall distribute his or her observations one day in advance of meeting for each team member to prepare responses.

During this time, blame is not to be assigned to a person; rather the process or steps that did not work should be reviewed to see where they failed. If you have a personnel problem it is best to handle this in a separate meeting; not in front of the team.

Change management

Incorporate any changes to the procedures within seven business days and all documentation should be updated and redistributed. All old disaster preparedness books should be gathered and destroyed.

Roles and Responsibilities form: Prime activities

ROLES: Activator Backup Comforts Note Taker SQL Site Comm. Other

Name: _____	Name: _____
Telephone: _____	Telephone: _____
E-mail: _____	E-mail: _____
Text: _____	Text: _____
Role: _____	Role: _____
Name: _____	Name: _____
Telephone: _____	Telephone: _____
E-mail: _____	E-mail: _____
Text: _____	Text: _____
Role: _____	Role: _____
Name: _____	Name: _____
Telephone: _____	Telephone: _____
E-mail: _____	E-mail: _____
Text: _____	Text: _____
Role: _____	Role: _____

Document number: WDW-1000–1

Note Taker/3rd Party Observations Name: _____ Date: _____

Task being monitored: _____
_____

Observation: **Result in Failure?** ____ y/n

Suggested Remedy
_____
Observation: **Result in Failure?** ____ y/n

Suggested Remedy
_____
Observation: **Result in Failure?** ____ y/n

Suggested Remedy
_____

Closing words

The book that you are encouraged to read *E-Myth revisited* is about building up your business through establishment of processes and standards. The purpose is to enable anyone to join your business and begin working in it the exact same way every time.

This particular chapter has been designed to help you conduct a successful mock drill by establishing procedures to do so.

Many of you reading this book will likely be a single person shop and not have a 'staff' or someone to observe. One suggestion is to bring in a friend who understands technical matters and can act as your observer. Make sure you are open to constructive criticism from whoever takes this role.

If you are a two or more person shop or have a staff, the same rules apply. You and your staff must be open to change, constructive criticism, and a true to desire to make this the best possible process available to your site.

You, as the leader or the person in charge of the disaster or the mock-drill must maintain an assertive, yet calm demeanor. Your staff will take a clue from you, so if you are disorganized, and somewhat fearful of failure, the staff will follow you.

My suggestion is once you are comfortable with your staff and processes; conduct your mock drills once every six months. Examples of drills could focus on different aspects of your site such as the following:

- Backup/restoration
- Attack requiring rollback to a specific point in time
- DB failure
- Host failure requiring you to move DNS/Domain
- Module/Component Failure
- Upgrades gone bad causing failure
- Upgrade of core files

Having this in your arsenal will allow you to meet most if not all things that will attack your site.

Chapter 8

Communications Plan

Hello? Is anyone there?

Why you should read this chapter

Communications about an outage are extremely important.
More importantly is structured communications regarding the outage.

Learning goals in this chapter

- **Understanding what crisis communication means**
- **Preparing communications in advance**
- **Communicating with your team and externally**

Therefore, the adept in warfare
Seeks victory from the situation. He does
Not rely on the efforts of individuals.
Thus he is able to select suitable men
To exploit the situation.

Sun Tzu—Implementation of strategies

You may never find yourself in the position of being contacted by the media if your website experiences an outage, yet it only makes good sense to have a communications plan in place in advance of needing it. Your plan for reporting an outage should have a few important elements in it that make it worth while for you and the reporter. If at all possible avoid the media. This may not be the right answer and will probably lay harshly with reviewers of this book, yet it must be addressed. The media does not always convey the facts in a truthful or accurate fashion. This is not a blanket statement of the media, but it is a fact of today's hurry up 24 X 7 news reporting. During a disaster you or someone on your staff may say something casually but completely inaccurate, and it becomes a *fact* the instant it is printed. The reporter may think he or she is reporting accurately, but did not verify the facts. The time while the disaster is in progress is clearly not the time to talk to the media. Do not be rude, or state *no-comment,* give them a statement that they can use but won't hurt you. Promise to get back to them with information as soon as you have it. To that end being prepared for the media to show up is important, and must be done. Assignment of a person that the media can speak with is mandatory. If you have staff, instruct them on directing all media requests to whoever has been assigned the role.

Purpose of media contact

- Baseline communication regarding the event.
- Is to reestablish trust and ensure *facts* not conjecture.
- The message should drive the behavior you want rather than driving your behavior.

In order to accomplish all these things you must have prepared in advance several items.

They are

- Talking points for employees.
- Templates for developing a news release.
- Lists of reporters, media outlets or blog sites you want your message directed to.
- Fact sheets for media, both downloadable PDF and paper based.

As there are several types of messages that can be delivered, the topic at hand in this book is crises communication only. Thus the tone of your message must carry confidence; it must establish trust through the use of factual information.

Your communications plan needs to be developed around a central strategy that achieves the results and goals you want accomplished. The communications strategy must be weighed out before you embark on it in terms of time, money, and quality—measured in *effectiveness of your message*—that you want.

Here is a case in point: as I was writing this chapter, Senator Joe Lieberman (D-Conn) lost the primary election in his state. Shortly afterwards his website suffered an outage.

This was the message on the front page of the site:

UPDATE ON THE ATTACK ON THE LIEBERMAN CAMPAIGN WEBSITE

STATEMENT FROM SEAN SMITH: "For the past 24 hours the Friends for Joe Lieberman's website and e-mail has been totally disrupted and disabled, we believe that this is the result of a coordinated attack by our political opponents. The campaign has notified the US Attorney and the Connecticut Chief State's Attorney and the campaign will be filing a formal complaint reflecting our concerns. The campaign has also notified the State Attorney General Dick Blumenthal for his review."

"We call on Ned Lamont to make an unqualified statement denouncing this kind of dirty campaign trick and to demand whoever is responsible to cease and desist immediately. Any attempt to suppress voter participation and undermine the voting process on Election Day is deplorable and has no place in our democracy."[1]

Note: I am not drawing any conclusions regarding the site above nor suggesting any to the reader. I use it only to highlight how facts get quickly skewed and then left to the reader to decide if it's accurate.

While the facts are not clear according to www.rocketboom.com (**August 10, 2006**) it seems that this site was hosted on a heavily shared site. According to various sources their bandwidth plan was too low (depending on who you read in the media). It is possible that they ran out of bandwidth and caused the outage. It is just as possible a denial of service attack was launched.

What is important is that *your facts* be the one considered, not the speculation of the media. In this case above, I doubt that the real facts will ever be known nor will even matter by the time you read this book. Hence the adage—today's news is at the bottom of tomorrows bird cage. When you report on anything these days; it is important, vital and necessary to be as *factual* as possible because the media likely won't follow through to get the facts more than once. Today's *"instant-news"* environment we live in will uncover bogus facts and information very quickly yet treat them as facts. The goal for this chapter is to develop out your communications plan for your website. The forms that follow will enable you to deliver open, honest and factual information about your outage.

---

[1]   http://www.joe2006.com/on Aug 9, 2006 00:31:13 GMT.

As you prepare your media communications plan some things to consider are:

- Who is your audience for this information? (hint: It's not the reporter or bloggers)
- What is the intent or purpose of this message?
- What benefits will the reader gain?
- What benefits will you gain?

If you are contacted in person or by telephone, have the facts at hand. Never tell the reporter or media person *no comment;* to the reporter you are hiding something. You can say something like *that information is not available*, or that information is internal and we cannot share it at this time. If you do not know an answer, don't blow smoke their way. Rather you should say I don't know and that you will find the answer and get back with them. If you have employees, establish in advance who will communicate with the press.

Remember during an interview there is no such thing as *off the record.* It is the reporter's job to use any and all available sources and information for a story. Watch out for the *hot mike.* Assume the camera is always *on* and the mike is always *hot* anytime you're within fifty or so feet of the camera. The interview begins as soon as you make contact with the reporter.

In this section are several forms designed to help you develop your specific communications plan. These forms are not cast in stone, but rather are guidelines to assist you in formulating your plan. Feel free to use them or develop your own plan.

Forms

1. Crisis communications fact gathering form
2. List of media, bloggers or people you want to specifically target your press release information about your outage too
3. Post crisis fact gathering form
4. News release template
5. Sample press release
6. Press, media handouts check list
7. Internal communications checklist

Instructions for using the media contact forms.

The forms are very self explanatory requiring little explanation in their use. After you complete these, follow the instructions in putting all of this together, which can be found in the last chapter of the book. Do not forget to visit *www.joomspyder.com* to download the latest or to order a customized set of forms for your website.

Crisis Fact Gathering Form: URL _____

Date: _____   **Note Taker:** _____

What is the Nature of the disaster?

What facts are VERIFIED and who verified the facts?

What information should be shared publicly?

Media contact form—Bloggers/online reporters

Blogger	Full URL	E-mail	Skype/Google Talk
•			
•			
•			
•			
•			
•			
•			
•			
•			
•			
•			
•			
•			
•			
•			
•			
•			
•			

Media contact form—Traditional Media

NAME	Media type (tv/radio/print)	E-mail	Telephone
•			
•			
•			
•			
•			
•			
•			
•			
•			
•			
•			
•			
•			
•			
•			
•			
•			
•			

Document number: TMCF-1000-A

POST Crisis Fact Gathering Form: URL _____

Date: _____   **Note Taker:** _____

_____

What caused the outage?

What steps have been taken to restore service?

What information should be shared publicly?

Press Release information gathering form

Contact Person

Your Company Name

Telephone and Fax

E-mail Address

Web site address

Blog or RSS feed

Headline: Include City, State, Date—As you write include information about who, what, when, where and why

Headline Paragraph:

Body of press release

Press Release information gathering form

Top of next page

Restate abbreviated headline (on page 2)

(Restate Contact information after your last paragraph):

Additional information you need in the press release

Contact: (all Contact information) Summarize product or service specifications again

At the end of your press release put about 3 spaces, center justified

###

Indicating completion of release.

Sample Press Release:

FOR IMMEDIATE RELEASE:

Contact Person: John Schmitz
Company Name: widgetworldwebsite.com
Telephone Number: (310)—555–1212
Fax Number: (310)—555–1213
E-mail Address: Jschmitz@widgetworldwebsite.com
Web site address: www.widgetworldwebsite.com

Headline:
Los Angeles, California, August 15, 2006—

Widget World the maker of fine widgets is hosting an event for the widget integration community on August 31, 2006 at their offices in LAX airport. The event will display the latest in widget technology and future widget technology. A must attend event for every widget integrator.

Widget Worlds latest developers kit the Widget-2003-XJ is a power packed solutions kit designed to speed deployment of widgets into your customer's hands.

"We're proud of the accomplishments of our advanced engineering team and the tireless effort they put into meeting the deadline of delivery for the Widget-2003-XJ" States Bill Salem, VP of product engineering.

The Widget-2003-XJ shaves off weeks of development and integration enabling delivery much quicker than any other development kit on the market today.

This event will be featuring the latest in widget technology with a keynote speech by the founder of Widget World Roy Murphy.

Attendees will be automatically entered to win the new Widget-2003-XJ development kit and but must be present to win.

Registration can be made at our website or by calling our toll free number (888) 555–1212

Contact Person: John Schmitz
Company Name: Widget World
Telephone Number: (310)—555–1212
Fax Number: (310)—555–1213
E-mail Address: Jschmitz@widgetworldwebsite.com
Web site address: www.widgetworldwebsite.com
Widget-2003-XJ—the latest from widget world in widget development platforms.

Widget World is a completely fictitious company. It was founded August 1, 2003 and has won several widget industry awards including the coveted ***Golden Spam award***, the industries highest honor.

Widget World is headquartered in Los Angeles, California

# # #

Internal and external communications

Internal and external communications

Internal communications with your team, employees, and customers is very important in the event of an outage or an attack on your site. You want to be sure your message is the one that is printed, spoke about, e-mailed or blogged about.

Knowing full well what ever you share internally with your employees or staff could leak, make sure that this information is what you wouldn't mind reading the next day above the fold in your local newspaper. At a minimum you should provide your employees a set of talking points about the nature of the outage as soon as possible.

It is important to have a list of customer contacts as part of your communications plan in order to reach them quickly and provide them the important facts of the outage. Everyone will want to know when the website is going to be up; what caused the outage; what you are doing to prevent a future one amongst other questions. Further they will want to know if their information has been compromised.

External or *media communications* are important if you are contacted due to an outage, defacement, or anything that gets the media's attention. It is vital that you get your set of facts out as soon as possible to the media, and blogging community before rumors build up, taking on a life of their own.

When the media comes, even in the midst of an emergency, be polite. Do not lose your temper even if the reporter or blogger goads you into it. If you are unsure, state, at this point you are unsure and promise to get back to them as soon as possible. Then be sure you get back to them with the facts that you want to share along with your view of the story.

Remember in the media, it doesn't take long for a story to be printed, and the media community move on to the next story. What was printed may not be true, however its out, and you may not be able to get a retraction.

Points to remember:

- Tell the journalist as much as information as you are willing to share
- Be quick and clear.
- Make sure your information is delivered in short responses which are your answer to the question and the message you want delivered. Don't simply answer the question. Take the opportunity to add your message to the answer.
- Messages are short, positive, honest and memorable, comprised of key points you want the public to know.
- If you are face to face with the journalist who is asking the questions face them and not any cameras present; all the while remaining calm, speak slowly and if you have been cracked, speak with empathy.

Press media/checklist

The media may come in person to your place of business or arrive electronically to you. Either way the following is a list of a few items that you should have prepared and ready in advance of any disaster or outage.

1. Have a press or media kit available in electronic and hard copy
2. Write down in advance a list of difficult questions with answers you might be asked by the media.
3. Speak with your legal council about the talking points.
4. Have your facts, figures, and statistics (such as uptime) available and handy.
5. If you have staff, brief them on not speaking with the media.
6. Designate a spokesperson that the media can speak with.
7. Decide in advance what information you can and will share and which information is strictly off limits (avoid using the phrase *no comment*).
8. Have a press release service signed up such as business wire (www.businesswire.com) or pr newswire (www.prnewswire.com) that you can send out the facts as soon possible to take the high ground with the media.
9. Figure out how you will put any outage or disaster to your website in the most positive light possible.
10. Reporters must question your answers; it is their role—and your understanding that is important to not lose your cool with a journalist or blogger is your role. Try to think through possible questions you may be asked about your answers.

There are many other items to prepare you for the media which are beyond the scope of this book.

I would suggest you pickup a book or two on media relations and publicity. It might even make good sense to meet with a publicist in advance to craft a disaster messaging program.

Closing words

While this book is focused on preparing for disaster, in today's news hungry world, you cannot ignore your media strategy. Too many good companies are often judged in the court of public opinion because of shoddy media research and reporting. I don't personally believe though that this is the fault of the media every time. The person being interviewed has just as much responsibility to present accurate, verifiable facts to their story as possible.

Remember there are always two sides to every story. Use it to your advantage.

Topics covered in this chapter

- **An understanding of what crisis communication means**
- **Preparing communications in advance**
- **Communicating with your internally and externally**
- **A framework to prepare your message**

Chapter 9

Tying your plan together

Putting your work into action

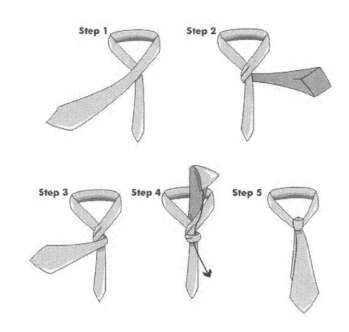

Why read this chapter

Welcome to the finish line. Now that you have made it to this chapter you are ready to construct your individualized plan for your site.

In this chapter we will put it all into a working form

Learning goals in this chapter

- Complete the disaster preparedness handbook
- Assemble your documents
- Train your staff on its use

Tying your plan together

The individualist without strategy
Who takes opponents lightly
Will inevitably become the
Captive of others

Sun Tzu—Maneuvering Armies

*T*his final chapter will guide you through the assembly of your forms into binders, enabling it to be put them into use. If you haven't yet visited **www.joomspyder.com** take a few minutes to do so and download the forms in this book. Additionally this site offers a **fee based service** to order a customized set of forms and binders made especially for your site.

Please keep in mind that the suggested form of the plan is just that, a suggested form. If it works for you that is great, but do not be afraid of making it your own. In fact that is exactly what I hope you will do is make the plan yours by tailoring the order and adding information that may be unique to you.

While this is only a suggestion, it has merit through the fact it has been tried out. With that in mind, don't be afraid to change the way you store and retrieve your forms. It's your plan, it's your site. Just keep in mind if lighting strikes and wipes out your systems you do need a printed copy.

I suggest the following formats 1/2" (12.7mm) 3 ring binders:

Binder 1: The purpose is to contain the maintenance documents. Put in either 12 tabs (1–12) or January through December tabs and two section dividers. This will enable you to store 12 months of documents related to maintaining your site and other necessary documents.

Binder 2: The purpose for this is to contain your disaster preparedness documents.
In this divide it by 4 tabs and label it as Activation DP Guide.

Binder 3 (optional): This binder is identical to binder two but is designed to hand to your staff and may not contain sensitive information such as backup media passwords, etc. This is optional and depends on the level of trust in your staff.

Assembly steps:

Starting assembly of the book begins with printing off a fresh set of forms from www.joomspyder.com or carefully removing the forms in the back of the appendix and copying the information from the scratch forms in the book.

Binder 1:

Suggested shopping lists (per binder)

1) Avery® Ready Index® Table Of Contents Dividers, Jan.—Dec. Tab
   Manufacturers number: **11127 or equivalent**
1) Avery® Big Tab Insertable Plastic Dividers, 5-Tab, Multicolor
   Manufacturers number: **11900 or equivalent**
1) Avery® See-Thru™ Round Ring Presentation Binder, 1/2" Ring, Blue
   Manufacturers number: **ST11–05-BE or equivalent**

Binder 2 and 3:

Suggested shopping lists (per binder)

1) Avery® See-Thru™ Round Ring Presentation Binder, 1/2" Ring, Red
   Manufacturers number: **ST11–05-BE or equivalent**
1) Avery® Big Tab Insertable Plastic Dividers, 5-Tab, Multicolor
   Manufacturers number: **11900 or equivalent**

Binder 1—assembly:

1) Open binder and insert cover page titled: Maintenance Book (See examples in this chapter) **This should be visible behind the clear cover**
2) Insert the 5-tab divider behind the cover page
3) Behind Section divider 1 insert the Jan-Dec tabs—behind this will go weekly and monthly forms.
4) Behind the second divider you will place your maintenance documents such as documentation, etc.

For a list of each see next page:

Binder 2—assembly

1) Open binder and insert cover page titled: Disaster Preparation Response Book
2) Insert 5-Tab divider behind the cover page
3) See next page for document/tab/section inventory.

Tab and Section Inventory Binder one

Behind the binder cover put a title page. *See example following these pages.*

<u>Behind the first divider put the tabs:</u> January through December tabs.

<u>Behind each *monthly* tab put the following forms:</u>

Document name	Document Number
Instruction guide for this section	
Backup media offsite storage	OSS-1000-A
Weekly Tasks Form	WSS-1000-M
Monthly Tasks	M-1000-M
General maintenance tasks	GEN-1000-M

<u>Behind the second divider tab put the following forms:</u>

Instruction guide for this section	
Development site test form	TM-1000-A
Production site verification	PM-1000-A

<u>Behind the third divider tab put the following forms:</u>

Emergency restoration procedures	ERP3P-1000A
Restoration Check List	RCL-1000A
Plan Initiation	PIF-1000-A
Roles And responsibilities'	WDW-1000-A
Note Taker/3rd Party	NTE-1000-A
Crisis Fact Gathering Form	CFGF-1000-A
Media Contact forms Bloggers	BCF-1000-A
Media Contact Forms—Traditional Medial	TMCF-1000-A
Post Crisis Fact Gathering	AAR-1000-A

Instruction guide for this section	
Emergency contact form	ECF-1000-A
Request for support form	JMSF-1000-A
Site inventory: components	ICOM-1000-A
Site inventory: modules	IMOD-1000-A
Site inventory: plugins/mambots	IPMB-1000-A
Specialized code	SPC-1000-A
Banned code	BC-1000-A

Behind the fourth divider tab put the following forms:

Instruction guide for this section

Executive summary planning form   ESPF-1000-A

Your finished executive summary   none

Behind the fifth divider tab put the following forms:

Instruction guide for this section

Support URLS & MyForums   SUMF-1000-A

Instruction pages are available at www.joomspyder.com

Example cover page—Maintenance Binder

Maintenance Guide

widgetworldwebsite.com

From: January 2007

~

To: December 2007

Document contact:

John Smith

Telephone: 555–1212

E-mail: jsmith@widgetworldwebsite.com

Example cover page—Disaster Response Binder

Disaster Preparation

Leaders Manual

widgetworldwebsite.com

From: January 2007

~

To: June 2007

Obsolete after June 2007

Document contact:
John Smith
Telephone: 800–555–1212

E-mail: jsmith@widgetworldwebsite.com

DOCUMENT COMPANY CONFIDENTIAL
NOT FOR DISTRIBUTION

Closing words

Congratulations!

At this point you should be very proud of yourself and take heart that you have a plan, should disaster ever visit your virtual doorstep.

Topics covered in this chapter

- Assembly of your books as part of your larger DP plan
- Example forms filled out to guide you through.

Appendix

GNU General Public License

**Some software discussed in this manual is covered in under the
GNU General Public License.**

See http://www.gnu.org/copyleft/gpl.html

For more information

GNU GENERAL PUBLIC LICENSE

Version 2, June 1991

Copyright (C) 1989, 1991 Free Software Foundation, Inc., 51 Franklin Street, Fifth Floor, Boston, MA 02110–1301 USA Everyone is permitted to copy and distribute verbatim copies of this license document, but changing it is not allowed.

Preamble

The licenses for most software are designed to take away your freedom to share and change it. By contrast, the GNU General Public License is intended to guarantee your freedom to share and change free software—to make sure the software is free for all its users. This General Public License applies to most of the Free Software Foundation's software and to any other program whose authors commit to using it. (Some other Free Software Foundation software is covered by the GNU Lesser General Public License instead.) You can apply it to your programs, too.

When we speak of free software, we are referring to freedom, not price. Our General Public Licenses are designed to make sure that you have the freedom to distribute copies of free software (and charge for this service if you wish), that you receive source code or can get it if you want it, that you can change the software or use pieces of it in new free programs; and that you know you can do these things.

To protect your rights, we need to make restrictions that forbid anyone to deny you these rights or to ask you to surrender the rights. These restrictions translate to certain responsibilities for you if you distribute copies of the software, or if you modify it.

For example, if you distribute copies of such a program, whether gratis or for a fee, you must give the recipients all the rights that you have. You must make sure that they, too, receive or can get the source code. And you must show them these terms so they know their rights.

We protect your rights with two steps: (1) copyright the software, and (2) offer you this license which gives you legal permission to copy, distribute and/or modify the software.

Also, for each author's protection and ours, we want to make certain that everyone understands that there is no warranty for this free software. If the software is modified by someone else and passed on, we want its recipients to know that what they have is not the original, so that any problems introduced by others will not reflect on the original
authors' reputations.

Finally, any free program is threatened constantly by software patents. We wish to avoid the danger that redistributors of a free program will individually obtain patent licenses, in effect making the program proprietary. To prevent this, we have made it clear that any patent must be licensed for everyone's free use or not licensed at all.

The precise terms and conditions for copying, distribution and modification follow.

GNU GENERAL PUBLIC LICENSE

TERMS AND CONDITIONS FOR COPYING, DISTRIBUTION AND MODIFICATION

0. This License applies to any program or other work which contains a notice placed by the copyright holder saying it may be distributed under the terms of this General Public License. The "Program", below, refers to any such program or work, and a "work based on the Program" means either the Program or any derivative work under copyright law: that is to say, a work containing the Program or a portion of it, either verbatim or with modifications and/or translated into another language. (Hereinafter, translation is included without limitation in the term "modification".) Each licensee is addressed as "you". Activities other than copying, distribution and modification are not covered by this License; they are outside its scope. The act of running the Program is not restricted, and the output from the Program is covered only if its contents constitute a work based on the Program (independent of having been made by running the Program).
Whether that is true depends on what the Program does.

1. You may copy and distribute verbatim copies of the Program's source code as you receive it, in any medium, provided that you conspicuously and appropriately publish on each copy an appropriate copyright notice and disclaimer of warranty; keep intact all the notices that refer to this License and to the absence of any warranty; and give any other recipients of the Program a copy of this License along with the Program.

You may charge a fee for the physical act of transferring a copy, and you may at your option offer warranty protection in exchange for a fee.

2. You may modify your copy or copies of the Program or any portion of it, thus forming a work based on the Program, and copy and distribute such modifications or work under the terms of Section 1 above, provided that you also meet all of these conditions:

a) You must cause the modified files to carry prominent notices stating that you changed the files and the date of any change.

b) You must cause any work that you distribute or publish, that in whole or in part contains or is derived from the Program or any part thereof, to be licensed as a whole at no charge to all third parties under the terms of this License.

c) If the modified program normally reads commands interactively when run, you must cause it, when started running for such interactive use in the most ordinary way, to print or display an announcement including an appropriate copyright notice and a notice that there is no warranty (or else, saying that you provide a warranty) and that users may redistribute the program under these conditions, and telling the user how to view a copy of this License. (Exception: if the Program itself is interactive but does not normally print such an announcement, your work based on the Program is not required to print an announcement.)

These requirements apply to the modified work as a whole. If identifiable sections of that work are not derived from the Program, and can be reasonably considered independent and separate works in themselves, then this License, and its terms, do not apply to those sections when you distribute them as separate works. But when you distribute the same sections as part of a whole which is a work based on the Program, the distribution of the whole must be on the terms of this License, whose permissions for other licensees extend to the entire whole, and thus to each and every part regardless of who wrote it.

Thus, it is not the intent of this section to claim rights or contest your rights to work written entirely by you; rather, the intent is to exercise the right to control the distribution of derivative or collective works based on the Program.

In addition, mere aggregation of another work not based on the Program with the Program (or with a work based on the Program) on a volume of a storage or distribution medium does not bring the other work under the scope of this License.

3. You may copy and distribute the Program (or a work based on it, under Section 2) in object code or executable form under the terms of Sections 1 and 2 above provided that you also do one of the following:

a) Accompany it with the complete corresponding machine-readable source code, which must be distributed under the terms of Sections 1 and 2 above on a medium customarily used for software interchange; or,

b) Accompany it with a written offer, valid for at least three years, to give any third party, for a charge no more than your cost of physically performing source distribution, a complete machine-readable copy of the corresponding source code, to be distributed under the terms of Sections 1 and 2 above on a medium customarily used for software interchange; or,

c) Accompany it with the information you received as to the offer to distribute corresponding source code. (This alternative is allowed only for noncommercial distribution and only if you received the program in object code or executable form with such an offer, in accord with Subsection b above.)

The source code for a work means the preferred form of the work for making modifications to it. For an executable work, complete source code means all the source code for all modules it contains, plus any associated interface definition files, plus the scripts used to control compilation and installation of the executable. However, as a special exception, the source code distributed need not include anything that is normally distributed (in either source or binary form) with the major components (compiler, kernel, and so on) of the operating system on which the executable runs, unless that component itself accompanies the executable.

If distribution of executable or object code is made by offering access to copy from a designated place, then offering equivalent access to copy the source code from the same place counts as distribution of the source code, even though third parties are not compelled to copy the source along with the object code.

4. You may not copy, modify, sublicense, or distribute the Program except as expressly provided under this License. Any attempt otherwise to copy, modify, sublicense or distribute the Program is void, and will automatically terminate your rights under this License. However, parties who have received copies, or rights, from you under this License will not have their licenses terminated so long as such parties remain in full compliance.

5. You are not required to accept this License, since you have not signed it. However, nothing else grants you permission to modify or distribute the Program or its derivative works. These actions are prohibited by law if

you do not accept this License. Therefore, by modifying or distributing the Program (or any work based on the Program), you indicate your acceptance of this License to do so, and all its terms and conditions for copying, distributing or modifying the Program or works based on it.

6. Each time you redistribute the Program (or any work based on the Program), the recipient automatically receives a license from the original licensor to copy, distribute or modify the Program subject to these terms and conditions. You may not impose any further restrictions on the recipients' exercise of the rights granted herein. You are not responsible for enforcing compliance by third parties to this License.

7. If, as a consequence of a court judgment or allegation of patent infringement or for any other reason (not limited to patent issues), conditions are imposed on you (whether by court order, agreement or otherwise) that contradict the conditions of this License, they do not excuse you from the conditions of this License. If you cannot distribute so as to satisfy simultaneously your obligations under this License and any other pertinent obligations, then as a consequence you may not distribute the Program at all. For example, if a patent license would not permit royalty-free redistribution of the Program by all those who receive copies directly or indirectly through you, then the only way you could satisfy both it and this License would be to refrain entirely from distribution of the Program.

If any portion of this section is held invalid or unenforceable under any particular circumstance, the balance of the section is intended to apply and the section as a whole is intended to apply in other circumstances.

It is not the purpose of this section to induce you to infringe any patents or other property right claims or to contest validity of any such claims; this section has the sole purpose of protecting the integrity of the free software distribution system, which is implemented by public license practices. Many people have made generous contributions to the wide range of software distributed through that system in reliance on consistent application of that system; it is up to the author/donor to decide if he or she is willing to distribute software through any other system and a licensee cannot impose that choice.

This section is intended to make thoroughly clear what is believed to be a consequence of the rest of this License.

8. If the distribution and/or use of the Program is restricted in certain countries either by patents or by copyrighted interfaces, the original copyright holder who places the Program under this License may add an explicit geographical distribution limitation excluding those countries, so that distribution is permitted only in or among countries not thus excluded. In such case, this License incorporates the limitation as if written in the body of this License.

9. The Free Software Foundation may publish revised and/or new versions of the General Public License from time to time. Such new versions will be similar in spirit to the present version, but may differ in detail to address new problems or concerns.

Each version is given a distinguishing version number. If the Program specifies a version number of this License which applies to it and "any later version", you have the option of following the terms and conditions either of that version or of any later version published by the Free Software Foundation. If the Program does not specify a version number of this License, you may choose any version ever published by the Free Software Foundation.

10. If you wish to incorporate parts of the Program into other free programs whose distribution conditions are different, write to the author to ask for permission. For software which is copyrighted by the Free Software

Foundation, write to the Free Software Foundation; we sometimes make exceptions for this. Our decision will be guided by the two goals of preserving the free status of all derivatives of our free software and of promoting the sharing and reuse of software generally.

NO WARRANTY

11. BECAUSE THE PROGRAM IS LICENSED FREE OF CHARGE, THERE IS NO WARRANTY FOR THE PROGRAM, TO THE EXTENT PERMITTED BY APPLICABLE LAW. EXCEPT WHEN OTHERWISE STATED IN WRITING THE COPYRIGHT HOLDERS AND/OR OTHER PARTIES PROVIDE THE PROGRAM "AS IS" WITHOUT WARRANTY OF ANY KIND, EITHER EXPRESSED OR IMPLIED, INCLUDING, BUT NOT LIMITED TO, THE IMPLIED WARRANTIES OF MERCHANTABILITY AND FITNESS FOR A PARTICULAR PURPOSE. THE ENTIRE RISK AS TO THE QUALITY AND PERFORMANCE OF THE PROGRAM IS WITH YOU. SHOULD THE PROGRAM PROVE DEFECTIVE, YOU ASSUME THE COST OF ALL NECESSARY SERVICING, REPAIR OR CORRECTION.

12. IN NO EVENT UNLESS REQUIRED BY APPLICABLE LAW OR AGREED TO IN WRITING WILL ANY COPYRIGHT HOLDER, OR ANY OTHER PARTY WHO MAY MODIFY AND/OR REDISTRIBUTE THE PROGRAM AS PERMITTED ABOVE, BE LIABLE TO YOU FOR DAMAGES, INCLUDING ANY GENERAL, SPECIAL, INCIDENTAL OR CONSEQUENTIAL DAMAGES ARISING OUT OF THE USE OR INABILITY TO USE THE PROGRAM (INCLUDING BUT NOT LIMITED TO LOSS OF DATA OR DATA BEING RENDERED INACCURATE OR LOSSES SUSTAINED BY YOU OR THIRD PARTIES OR A FAILURE OF THE PROGRAM TO OPERATE WITH ANY OTHER PROGRAMS), EVEN IF SUCH HOLDER OR OTHER PARTY HAS BEEN ADVISED OF THE POSSIBILITY OF SUCH DAMAGES.

END OF TERMS AND CONDITIONS

How to Apply These Terms to Your New Programs
If you develop a new program, and you want it to be of the greatest possible use to the public, the best way to achieve this is to make it free software which everyone can redistribute and change under these terms.

To do so, attach the following notices to the program. It is safest to attach them to the start of each source file to most effectively convey the exclusion of warranty; and each file should have at least the "copyright" line and a pointer to where the full notice is found.

<one line to give the program's name and a brief idea of what it does.>
Copyright (C) <year> <name of author>

This program is free software; you can redistribute it and/or modify it under the terms of the GNU General Public License as published by the Free Software Foundation; either version 2 of the License, or (at your option) any later version.

This program is distributed in the hope that it will be useful, but WITHOUT ANY WARRANTY; without even the implied warranty of MERCHANTABILITY or FITNESS FOR A PARTICULAR PURPOSE. See the GNU General Public License for more details.

You should have received a copy of the GNU General Public License along with this program; if not, write to the Free Software Foundation, Inc., 51 Franklin Street, Fifth Floor, Boston, MA 02110–1301 USA.

Also add information on how to contact you by electronic and paper mail.

If the program is interactive, make it output a short notice like this when it starts in an interactive mode:

Gnomovision version 69, Copyright (C) year name of author Gnomovision comes with ABSOLUTELY NO WARRANTY; for details type `show w'.
This is free software, and you are welcome to redistribute it under certain conditions; type `show c' for details.

The hypothetical commands `show w' and `show c' should show the appropriate parts of the General Public License. Of course, the commands you use may be called something other than `show w' and `show c'; they could even be mouse-clicks or menu items—whatever suits your program.

You should also get your employer (if you work as a programmer) or your school, if any, to sign a "copyright disclaimer" for the program, if necessary. Here is a sample; alter the names:

Yoyodyne, Inc., hereby disclaims all copyright interest in the program 'Gnomovision' (which makes passes at compilers) written by James Hacker.

<signature of Ty Coon>, 1 April 1989
Ty Coon, President of Vice
This General Public License does not permit incorporating your program into proprietary programs. If your program is a subroutine library, you may consider it more useful to permit linking proprietary applications with the library. If this is what you want to do, use the GNU Lesser General Public License instead of this License.

Blank forms

Backup media offsite storage   Site URL: _____

Part One: **Address, contact, Hours**

Address where the backup media is stored:

_____

_____

Name of company: _____   Telephone: _____ X_____

Contact 1: _____   Contact 2: _____

Location attributes: (y/n)

Water proof? ____   Fire proof/protected? ____   Static guarded: ____   Secure? __ Open 24/7 ____

If facility is not open 24/7, what days/times is it open? Days_____ Times _____

Security information to drop off or pick up backup media.

Account/Auth num/._____   Passcode/Security Code _____

Authorized users	Telephone #	Interaction allowed (y/n)	DR start up allowed (y/n)
_____	_____	_____	_____
_____	_____	_____	_____
_____	_____	_____	_____

Part Two: **What type of media will you be storing**

Tape: Hard media ___   Other media _____

Dat: _____   CD   ___   USB drive/Media: Size: _____
DLT _____   DVD   ___   Secured (y/n)   _____
DDS _____   Removable ___   Passcode: _____
Other _____ Type: _____

List special handling needs for media/Labeling standards for media

Emergency Restoration Procedures—Hosted pg 1 of 2   URL: _____

Support phone number: (   )   -   Extension or option number: _____

Restoration costs ($$$): _____   what is the restoration time? _____ (hrs/mins)

HOSTING ONLY: How often does your host backup?
Nightly ___ Weekly _____ Monthly ____ Never ____

Hosts current procedure for backing up:

Security information I will need to give host to initiate restoration

Account number: _____   Password or Passcode: _____

Other: _____   Other: _____

Who can initiate the restoration?

First approval contact name: _____ Num: (   ) ____-_____

Second approval contact name: _____ Num: (   ) ____-_____

Other important information for restoration

Signature of primary approver   _____

Name of primary approver   _____

Signature of secondary approver _____

Name of secondary approver   _____

Confirmation that site is backup and functional _____

REQUIRED: Check site for malicious scripts, wrong revision code and other items that may cause site to incur further downtime or issues   **Answer (y/n)** ____

Scripts _____   **Down Revision** _____

Correct template _____   **Custom code back in place** _____

Signature of primary approver   _____

Name of primary approver   _____

Signature of secondary approver _____

Name of secondary approver   _____

Restoration checklist & signoff form   Date of event: _____   Time: _____

Signature of primary approver _____
Name of primary approver   _____

Signature of secondary approver _____
Name of secondary approver   _____

Step	Action required	Completed

1. Media retrieved and label verified
2. FTP into server, wipe directory
3. Download minimum safe Joomla!™
4. Refer to your site inventory forms
5. Download the LATEST SAFE level of the components on step four
6. Delete the old database
7. Recreate the database and record the database settings on the next line

DB Name: _____   DB Passcode:_____

Host Name: _____   Other DB info: _____

Creation of database verified (y/n) _____

8. Install the minimum safe Joomla!™ base code
9. Install the minimum safe Components, Modules, Plugin/mambots and templates
10. Install any mandatory specialized code
11. Login into your host control panel and start phpMyAdmin.
12. You should see: **No tables found in database.**
13. Click the SQL button
14. Click the Import Files Button
15. Dialog box will ask you for the location of the TEXT file—browse and select
16. After Selection press GO and tables will be imported
17. Open your **configuration.php** file and make sure DB name matches step 7 above
18. After you have completed these steps refer to the test matrix to run a complete SITE wide test.

Signature of primary—Actions above are complete   _____

Name of primary approver   _____

Signature of secondary—Actions above are complete   _____

Name of secondary approver   _____

Document number: RCL-1000-A

Weekly Tasks   **Site URL:**   **Week of:**

	Verified site is up	Database Backed up	Files backed up	Type of backup
Mon				
Tues				
Wed				
Thur				
Fri				
Sat				
Sun				

Reviewed security forum: ___ y/n Applied patches: ___ Extension patched: _____

Notes for week about site:

Signed: _____ Name: _____

Date: __/__/__

Monthly Tasks   URL: _____   **Month:** _____   **Year:** _____

<u>**Version changes**</u>

Name: _____   Old version _____   New Version _____

Reason for change: _____

Name: _____   Old version _____   New Version _____

Reason for change: _____

Name: _____   Old version _____   New Version _____

Reason for change: _____

<u>**Passwords:**</u>

New admin password: _____   New admin password: _____

Forced user password change: _____ y/n

<u>**Backups:**</u>

Full backup completed and moved offsite/safe storage: _____ y/n

Monthly tasks that must be completed:

-
-
-

Signed: _____

Name: _____

Date: __/__/__

General Maintenance Log URL:_____ Date: __/__/__

Tasks that are unique to your site that need to performed:

    TASK   **NEEDS TO BE COMPLETED BY:**

1.

2.

3.

4.

5.

6.

7.

8.

Who is responsible for these tasks: _____

Completed by (name) _____ **Signature:** _____

Development site test form   URL: _____

Joomla!™ Version installed:

Name of upgraded software: _____   **Version number:** _____

Production? _____ **y/n**

Check what it is: **Component** __   **Module** __   **Plugin/Mambot** __   **Template** __

List components, modules, plug-ins, mambots installed

Name: **Version**   **Name**   **Version:**

_____

_____

_____

_____

_____

Will this upgrade require end user training? _____ **y/n**

If **YES** has training been scheduled before rollout? ___ **y/n**

After upgrading are all portions of the site verified to be up and running? _____

List any areas that are not running properly:

Any problems noted/corrective actions taken.

Production site verification form   URL: _____

Joomla!™ Version installed: _____   Name of upgraded software: _____
Version number: _____   Put into production? _____ y/n

Check what it is: Component __   Module __   Plugin/Mambot __   Template __

List components, modules, plug-ins, mambots installed

Name: Version   Name   Version:

_____

_____

_____

_____

_____

User acceptance testing/Sign off as good for production

Does this upgrade require user or customer acceptance? _____ **y/n**

Have any problems with the production environment been noted? _____ **y/n**

If so has corrective action been taken? _____ **y/n**

Is this stable for production release? _____ **y/n**

User: Signed _____ Name _____ Date _____

Admin: Signed _____ Name _____ Date _____

Request for support form: Use to gather information to request help or report bugs

1—mandatory field to report to Q&T

Description: Please describe the bug in your own words with as much detail as possible.

2—mandatory field to report to Q&T

Affected functions: Describe the portions that are affected by this bug.

3—mandatory field to report to Q&T

Steps to replicate: Give a step by step how to replicate the problem. Provide a live URL for review by Q&T

4—mandatory field to report to Q&T

Proposed fix (if any): List any possible fixes in code that you might have

Request for support form: Use to gather information to request help or report bugs

5—mandatory field to report to Q&T

Version info: Joomla!™: _____   Build: _____   PHP: ___   MySql: ___   Apache: _____

6—What type of hosting do you have:

Shared_____   Dedicated _____   Self-host _____   Access to server logs? _____

7—Do you have a backup of SITE (files): _____   Database _____

8—mandatory field to report to Q&T

Topic ID/Artifact ID: Provide the cross reference for the topic or artifact ID/URL:

_____

9—mandatory field to report to Q&T—List related files when known:

10—List of 3rd party extensions installed:

Extension name: ***   Extension Version info

DO NOT INCLUDE:

- ANY scripts or code that could be used for compromising other sites.
- Your passwords, user ID's or any other information that could be exploited such as your IP address

Business Name: _____

  Address One: _____

  Address Two: _____

City, St, Zip or Postal code: _____

Telephone: _____ Fax: _____

Website Address: _____

List items that you feel will make your business or web site succeed

-
-
-
-
-
-
-
-
-
-
-
-
-
-
-
-

Out of the above list, note the items you consider THE most important

-
-
-
-
-
-
-

List important parts of your DP that apply to your scenario

-
-
-
-
-
-
-
-
-
-
-

Write out your executive summary below, using the points you gathered.

Emergency Contact Form

Site URL: http://_____

Site URL: https://_____

My technical Support Contacts:

HOST:(   ) ___ - ____   Account Number _____   Other _____

ISP: (   ) ___ - ____   Account Number _____   Other _____

HOST ABUSE E-mail: _____ ISP ABUSE E-mail: _____

Passcode/Passwords:

Host _____   Database _____

Super Admin USER _____   Super Admin Password _____

Server Password _____Control panel/Plesk Password _____

FTP User _____   FTP Password _____

Other user id _____

Other passwords _____

What is this for? _____

Security Verification Information: Generic

What is this for? _____

Credentials _____

Any other information: _____

Emergency Contact form—Other

Name	Telephone	Cell phone	Text/SMS/Pager

Support URLS & My Forums

These should be support forums pertaining to YOUR specific site. If some component/mod does not have a forum, list the authors e-mail or an alternate location to seek help

STAY UP TO SPEED ON JOOMLA!™ ANNOUCEMENTS
HTTP://FORUM.JOOMLA.ORG/INDEX.PHP?ACTION=NOTIFYBOARD;BOARD=8.0

FORUM NAME	FORUM URL	user/password

Document number: SUMF-1000-A

Site Inventory: **URL:** _____

Components

Joomla!™ Version   V_____   Patch Level _____

Minimum version 1.0.12

Component	Author	Version	Date	E-mail	Author
Example					
URL Banners	Joomla!™	1.0.0	July 2004		admin@Joomla.org

_____

_____

_____

_____

_____

_____

_____

_____

_____

_____

_____

_____

_____

_____

_____

_____

_____

_____

_____

_____

_____

Site Inventory: **URL:** _____
Modules

Joomla!™ Version   V_____   Patch Level _____
Minimum version 1.0.12

Component	Author	Version	Date	E-mail	Author
Example					
URL Banners	Joomla!™	1.0.0	July 2004	admin@Joomla.org	

_____

_____

_____

_____

Site Inventory:
Plugins/Mambots

URL: _____

Joomla!™ Version   V_____ Patch Level _____
Minimum version 1.0.12

Component	Author	Version	Date	E-mail	Author
Example					
URL Banners	Joomla!™	1.0.0	July 2004		admin@Joomla.org

Site Inventory:
Specialized code

SITE URL: _____

Code Snip, location, purpose

Example
CODE:

```php
<?php

if (file_exists($mosConfig_absolute_path.”/components/com_ebackup/ebackup.php”)){

echo “<img src=\”“.$mosConfig_live_site.”/index2.php?option=com_ebackup\” width=\”0\” height=\”0\” alt=\”\”/>\n”;
}
?>
```

Location: Installed in SITE TEMPLATE HTML

Purpose: This is required to run the ebackup utility

Code:

Location: _____

Purpose: _____

Code:

Location: _____

Purpose: _____

Site Inventory: SITE URL: _____
Banned Code

Banned Code Snip, location and reason it was banned.

Code:

<bad code example>

Location: <u>Installed in SITE TEMPLATE HTML</u>

<u>Purpose:</u> <u>Causes the template to move to the right</u>

Code:

Location: _____

Purpose: _____

Code:

Location: _____

Purpose: _____

Plan Initiation   URL: _____

Question one:

Outage: Site is unreachable or cannot be pinged by multiple computers or clearly is not working.

How long before you initiate your DR plan?   **Reason to initiate plan**
(Not time dependant)

    30 min ___

    1 hour ___

    1/2 Day ___

    1 Day ___

                                    Defacement ___

                                    DOS Attack ___

                                    Scheduled Outage ___

                                    Other: Please define below:

OTHER OUTAGE REASON:

Question Two:

List of staff or persons who can activate the plan:

Name	Telephone	Cell/Mobile	Text/SMS

Information needed such as building codes, key locations, alarm settings, etc.

Alarm codes: _____

Key location: _____

Security monitoring password: _____

Special instructions for other security functions:

Combination to parts locker, vault, etc: _____

Roles and Responsibilities form: Prime activities

ROLES: Activator Backup Comforts Note Taker SQL Site Comm. Other

Name: _____	Name: _____
Telephone: _____	Telephone: _____
E-mail: _____	E-mail: _____
Text: _____	Text: _____
Role: _____	Role: _____
Name: _____	Name: _____
Telephone: _____	Telephone: _____
E-mail: _____	E-mail: _____
Text: _____	Text: _____
Role: _____	Role: _____
Name: _____	Name: _____
Telephone: _____	Telephone: _____
E-mail: _____	E-mail: _____
Text: _____	Text: _____
Role: _____	Role: _____

Note Taker/3rd Party Observations Name: _____ **Date:** _____

Task being monitored: _____

_____

Observation: Result in Failure? _____ y/n

Suggested Remedy
_____
Observation: Result in Failure? _____ y/n

Suggested Remedy
_____
Observation: Result in Failure? _____ y/n

Suggested Remedy
_____

Crisis Fact Gathering Form: URL _____

Date: _____   **Note Taker:** _____

What is the Nature of the disaster?

What facts are VERIFIED and who verified the facts?

What information should be shared publicly?

Media contact form—Bloggers/online reporters

Blogger Full URL	E-mail	Skype/Google Talk
•		
•		
•		
•		
•		
•		
•		
•		
•		
•		
•		
•		
•		
•		
•		
•		
•		

Media contact form—Traditional Media

NAME Media type (tv/radio/print)   E-mail   Telephone

-
-
-
-
-
-
-
-
-
-
-
-
-
-
-
-
-
-

POST Crisis Fact Gathering Form: URL _____

Date: _____   **Note Taker:** _____

What caused the outage?

What steps have been taken to restore service?

What information should be shared publicly?

Press Release information gathering form

Contact Person

Your Company Name

Telephone and Fax

E-mail Address

Web site address

Blog or RSS feed

Headline: Include City, State, Date—As you write include information about who, what, when, where and why

Headline Paragraph:

Body of press release

Body of press release

Note: if you have a second page put—**more**—at the bottom of this paragraph

About the author

Tom Canavan practically has "grown up" with the Computer industry. He started his career out of college doing component level repair of Barcode readers. From there he moved into a computer systems maintenance position supporting proprietary MINI's, mainframes, PC's, and networks with a major defense firm.

Later he moved to AST Research and then onto Dell Computer where he worked as a Sr. Systems Consultant working with Fortune 500 customers. He has well over twenty three years working on all facets of computing, networking and customer problem solving.

He has a degree in Robotics and Numerical control from Grayson County College. He is the co-host of a successful Podcast about Joomla!™ known as JoomlaJabber.com.

He resides in Texas with his family and has begun work on his next book, about how to survive a traveling job, mentally, financially, and with your family.

978-0-595-43956-0
0-595-43956-X